INSIDER SECRETS TO

DIAMOND DEALING

How Real Money Is Made

D1519261

MAXIMILLIAN S. CALLAHAN

PALADIN PRESS
BOULDER, COLORADO

Insider Secrets to Diamond Dealing:
How Real Money is Made
by Maximillian S. Callahan

Copyright © 1996 by Maximillian S. Callahan

ISBN 0-87364-876-5
Printed in the United States of America

Published by Paladin Press, a division of
Paladin Enterprises, Inc., P.O. Box 1307,
Boulder, Colorado 80306, USA.
(303) 443-7250

Direct inquiries and/or orders to the above address.

CONTENTS

To my writing mentors, J.T., L.C., and T.P.—and to my editor, Karen Pochert, who corrected all the bad writing habits the other three tried to drum out of me.

FOREWORD

PLINY THE ELDER, IN THE FIRST CENTURY OF THE COM-
MON ERA, called diamonds "the most valuable, not only
of precious stones, but of all things in this world." Who
among us can argue with Pliny? A diamond is a piece of
rock, a lump of carbon so small that I can send one
through the mail using a single postage stamp, and yet so
valuable that it would pay for purchasing, not to mention furnishing, a fine home in the United States. In
other parts of the world the value of even a single small
stone may be many times the total of wages a worker
could hope to receive throughout his entire life.

Anything so valuable gets creative juices flowing in
some people. It starts palms itching. The thought of that
kind of money makes people want to get on the band-
wagon for the golden bucks they feel are just over the
hill, in that pot that lies at the point where the end of the
rainbow touches earth.

So why doesn't everybody give up jobs at the local
fast-food restaurant or take a long vacation from a rust-

belt factory and plunge into the world of diamond dealers and smugglers?

Well . . . the diamond business isn't that easy—which is not to say that it is that hard, either. It's more correct to call it confusing. And it takes a certain type of person to become involved—and survive—in a cutthroat world where the businessmen in silk suits are arguably even tougher than the ruffian smugglers who deal in drugs and people.

The type of person who can survive, and even thrive, in the diamond business is someone who is gregarious and outgoing. He is a person who can make friends easily and get them to talk about themselves and the things they know about. But that same person has to be taciturn enough to know when not to talk, what not to say, while behaving in such a way that people think he is wise rather than speechless.

The people who profit from this trade seem even harder than the stones they sell—and remember that diamonds are known as the hardest natural material in the world. In this book we'll explore the yin and yang of the business, for the world of diamonds is a business. It is a business that has about the same relationship to the mushy sentiment spread across the pages of bridal magazines that a graffiti artist has to a Michaelangelo or a Da Vinci.

The diamond business has profit margins, startup companies, and monopolies. There are pick-and-shovel men and executive boards. There is boredom galore, but there is also what some might call excitement. And there is certainly danger.

This book has been carefully put together to start you on the way to acquiring the absolute basics of the business. And any examination of the diamond business demands a careful look at smuggling. A large part of the world's diamond stocks is smuggled at one time or another. Equipment requirements of the diamond trader, such as loupes and gauges, will be referenced as needed.

Many basic diamond terms, such as the parts of a diamond, are covered in the text. There is also a glossary at the end dealing with the terminology and argot of the business. Pay close attention to that; it may be the most important part of this book. Many phrases that are not covered in the text are found there. Except for diamond couriers, who simply pick up a package at one place and leave it at another, no one has any chance of success in this business if he doesn't know the language that is peculiar to the diamond trade. A failure to understand the terms identifies the person as a neophyte. It is like wearing a sign saying "take me for all I'm worth." Given the cutthroat attitude that exists in the diamond business, it's a sure bet someone will.

Finally, there are four terms you need to know better than your own name. You'll have to learn to recite the "Four Cs" in your sleep:

- Color
- Cut
- Clarity
- Carat weight

These are the four things that go into a diamond's value. They all work together. None is really more important than the other. A baseball-sized diamond, but one that is so flawed and of such poor clarity that it grades out as an industrial stone, may well be little more than a paperweight that will make a good conversation piece.

Although this book will cover much of what you need to know about the cold, hard business of diamonds, there is no sense in pretending that it will teach you everything. No one learns how to drive a car or fly a plane simply by reading a book—you have to press the pedal and learn how to lean out a throttle. The diamond business is a hands-on business, but, most important, it is a brain-on business.

This, and every other book ever written about diamonds, is only a starting point. If you're interested in going further in this business, you'll have to cajole others to teach you; you'll need to work for a chance to learn. You'll be knocking on jewelers' doors in July asking them to keep you in mind for a sales position during the always busy Christmas season, when they'll need part-time help. In the diamond business, everybody has to serve an apprenticeship and learn from their mistakes. Should you go on, you too will have to make your costly errors as you negotiate the learning curve.

But there is one mistake you should never make: never admit to smuggling so much as a button. Never. Ever.

I've never smuggled anything. You haven't either. Remember, if you feel an overwhelming desire to confess your shame and guilt, you can admit to killing Lizzie Borden's parents when Customs officials interrogate you. But remember, you never smuggled anything. Never. Ever. If you ever admit to so much as smuggling a matchstick, you'll be in the kind of trouble that neither this book, nor any other, can get you out of.

AN INTRODUCTION— PEOPLE, PLACES, AND POLITICS

THE DIAMOND TRADE IS A BIG BUSINESS. In a normal year, world production of diamonds averages 100 million carats a year, though only about 15 percent of this is in gem-quality stones.

The gemstones are sorted into about 5,000 different categories. They are valued on the basis of size, clarity, shape, and color. Retail sales of polished-diamond jewelry, another market entirely, totals perhaps $40 billion annually. It's not only a big business, it's a burgeoning business, a growth industry. In the mid-1990s, diamond jewelry sales worldwide totaled about $42 billion, up from $21.1 billion a decade before.

The diamond trade is as hard as it is big. It is even harder than the stones that are traded, cleaved, bruted, and polished. The would-be diamond smuggler or self-declared diamond dealer who wanders into this world and is not armed with extensive knowledge is certain to regret it. Some who try to go head to head with dictators and criminal cartels, such as the Russian mafia, don't live long enough to reflect on their mistakes.

"Diamonds are forever" was a phrase that a public relations whiz kid pitched in the 1930s to improve diamond sales during the Depression slump. The phrase ignored the reality of both facts and history, but it worked then. It still sells diamonds now. While the sales pitch may not be true, and diamonds are not forever, the reality is that the diamond business is forever dangerous.

As with most things in life, there's a right way and a wrong way to do things in the diamond business. For instance, time plays a role in the diamond merchant's work. Time is one factor that movers of stones have to be aware of. Christmas is a pivotal diamond season and affects the trade. As an example, there is always a post-Christmas restocking demand in the United States, which is the world's largest market for polished stones. There is heavy demand, and heavy traffic, in fashioned stones before Christmas. The merchant must be prepared to deal with that rush and be ready to take a "vacation" during the slack times. For some dealers and movers of diamonds, it is important to know that DeBeers "sights," or private offerings, of uncut stones tend to be concentrated at the beginning of the year and then trail off. In that way, people can plan the year, with the stones from the sights in January and February appearing as polished goods in the summer so that they will be in the shops for Christmas.

As is true in other aspects of life, it is fair to say that in the diamond business the average person can't make much money. There are no such things as legitimate get-rich-quick schemes. Lose your shirt, even lose your freedom or your life—that's what can happen to the man or woman on the street who tries to crack the code on some aspects of this business. It takes a special kind of person, a special kind of determination, and a special kind of knowledge to succeed.

The diamond trade, both legal and illicit, is based to a great extent on geology, politics, and economics. In general, the facts of where diamonds come from, as well as where they go to, involve a mix of the three. This recipe for an "information stew" is important to understand, however, because it sets the diamond dealer's table of supply and demand.

Sellers and smugglers of diamonds always have to take into account the buyer, and the buyers are mostly found in the industrialized and industrializing world.

For instance, Japan and the United States have the economic wherewithal needed to be a major user of gem diamonds. These countries have political and social systems that encourage such use. However, any time there are major stock market drops, moves to impose higher taxes on luxury goods, or efforts to pile additional taxes on the incomes of rich people, the diamond market can and does fall like a stone. In the polished-diamonds market, the United States has remained the main buyer despite the recent economic roller coaster ride. In Japan, when the fall of the Nikkei index led to a loss of consumer confidence, the economic battering negatively affected the sale of all luxury goods, including polished diamonds. Watching global economics becomes one of the main jobs of every international diamond dealer and mover.

Apart from their aesthetic beauty and value, diamonds have a very practical side. They can be used to make wire for industry and to sharpen machine tools. Their importance to industry is so great that they have been a major item in the strategic stockpiles of many First World nations, though concern over a lack of industrial diamonds has declined with the development of synthetic stones. Nonetheless, some diamond movers and traders have found that there can be a good niche market in dealing industrial-grade stones.

First World countries aren't the only diamond users. China is one diamond market that is bucking the global trend; it is experiencing dramatic growth in sales from a low base. While China remains an anomaly in terms of markets, it is being watched by diamond movers of all types with intense interest. A land of more than a billion people, China, many speculate, will turn into one of the world's major markets at the millennium.

Second and Third World countries that are attempting to industrialize, or reindustrialize, also need lesser-quality diamonds for a variety of uses. Industrialized and industrializing countries, east and west, are thus a magnet for certain types and grades of diamonds.

Geology is another key to the diamond trade. Some countries that have very little use for diamonds—nations where the people would be better off if they got sufficient quantities of food and textiles out of their land instead of loads of inedible stones—are sources of diamonds. These countries serve as the first stepping stone on the long path that a diamond takes as it travels from clay envelope to glittering jewel at the opera. And that's all based on geology.

South Africa is often thought of as *the* source of diamonds. But the reality is that there is any number of sources, from malaria-ridden Zaire and Angola to the frozen wastes of Russia and Canada. And the creative juices of would-be smugglers and traders are flowing in places like Angola, Zaire, Canada, and Russia. So too is the flow of diamonds——or soon will be.

PEOPLE

BOTH DEALERS AND SMUGGLERS OF DIAMONDS DO IT FOR A COUPLE OF VERY GENERAL REASONS: they expect to make money and receive satisfaction from it. But diamond smuggling, in particular, is done for a variety of more specific reasons.

Greed is one. And in the United States there isn't much reason to smuggle other than sheer greed: the country's American diamond dealers are an obvious group to profit from smuggling. Their reasons almost invariably involve greed.

When U.S. dealers smuggle they are almost always involved in a tax-avoidance scheme. The diamond fraternity—and it is literally a fraternity; women are systematically excluded—seldom does its own "mule" work. Diamond dealers rarely put themselves at personal risk. When they want to smuggle in goods physically, they hire others to take the risks. They will normally set up the purchase abroad and simply use couriers to carry their illicit parcels. These couriers are often aircraft flight crews traveling international routes.

Actually, most diamond dealers usually prefer using semilegal invoicing scams, which are safer than employing couriers who will physically smuggle in the goods. Even if the scams are detected by the authorities, that seldom results in anything worse than the loss of the stones. It's hard for prosecutors to prove that someone intended to misidentify stones if they are off only one or two clarity grades or a color grade. A couple of clarity and color grades involve subtle, and often visually imperceptible, physical differences that make a great deal of difference in both price and declared value at a border. But juries in the United States, working under the rule that guilt has to be proven beyond a reasonable doubt, find it easy to believe that someone else—a diamond grader somewhere—had a bad night and simply made mistakes in detecting differences in diamonds. That is especially true since these are differences that the jurors can't perceive. A good defense lawyer can generally throw up enough questions, raise enough doubts, that most people engaging in well-thought-out invoice smuggling will never be convicted. It's well to keep in mind that prosecutors in the United States seldom pursue cases they can't win. That's the bottom line that makes invoicing techniques relatively safe.

Let's make one thing clear here: Without having a diamond dealer available at some point in the chain, smuggling is always a losing scheme. The diamond smuggler, of whatever type, either has to be a dealer or have access to a dealer somewhere to dispose of the "submarine goods."

As a result of that clear fact, the importance of knowing the argot of the diamond-dealing fraternity cannot be overemphasized. It is a tight fraternity. The knowledge of diamonds and their specialized language is the password. If you don't know the code, you're in for an icy reception.

Drug dealers also do some diamond smuggling, though surprisingly little considering the amount of "value"—some call it money—they need to move from one place to another. And value is an important concept in diamond dealing and smuggling. If he doesn't have an almost intuitive understanding of what value is, the would-be diamond dealer or smuggler might as well go to Las Vegas and play the slots—it's a better and safer way to spend time and money.

Value is the way that people store work or effort. Money, also called currency, is one form of value, but there are many currencies that have no real value. Inflation is a fact of life that decreases value in currencies. Drugs, too, have "value" and are traded for other things that are "valuable." However, the value of drugs is often unstable, depending on their availability at any given time. Historically, diamonds and gold have represented a fairly stable measure of value. As a result, over the millennia diamonds and gold have become commodities that can be transported from one place to the other with the expectation that a week, a month, or a year later they will have relatively the same value. For that reason, both diamonds and gold are recognized as a sort of international supercurrency. Interestingly, most drug dealers find the downside of diamond smuggling—the need to have expertise to purchase the stones and to convert the stones to cash at the other end—to be too much of a hassle. Drug dealers have a gambler's mind set that usually brings them to take their chances with movements of cash or with sophisticated money-laundering schemes.

Refugees, or people other than drug smugglers facing stringent currency transfer restrictions, are perhaps the best candidates to successfully engage in nonprofessional diamond smuggling. That is because, although the risk of getting caught at diamond smuggling is often tolerably low, the chance for a nonprofessional to recover the total value at the sale end of the pipeline is equally low. Refugees aren't trying to get rich; they're simply trying to salvage any small part of their lives and life-style. They seldom have any outside help and must rely on their wits, good sense, and luck. Refugees don't need to make a profit, or even have a 100-percent recovery of value, to count their effort as a success. And it is well that is the case. The diamond market is structured in such a way that disposing of smuggled diamonds at a profit is practically impossible for the nonprofessional (i.e., someone who is not a member of the diamond fraternity). There is a great deal of truth in that famous scene from *Casablanca* where a refugee pleads for just a little more money and is told "Madame, diamonds are a drug on the market right now."

There are other people, though not refugees, who use diamonds as means of evading currency export restrictions. And there have been agents of some governments who carry diamonds as a means of transporting value. During the Cold War, government agents for the world powers did make some payments and money transfers through smuggled diamonds. In all honesty, the conversion process is, and was, so onerous that this method of value transfer is pretty far down the preferred list. In addition, diamonds are often traceable. Diamond experts, looking at a selection of stones from the same location, can often tell the point of origin. For instance, Russian diamonds tend to stand out when experts view them because of the type of inclusions (internal flaws) in the stones. During the Cold War, the former Soviet Union sometimes used diamonds for financing guerrilla wars abroad. But even the Soviets found that there were difficulties inherent in the conversion of diamonds to needed cash.

Diamonds normally must be converted to some other form of value before they can be put to use by political or insurgent groups. Few arms dealers, for instance, will take diamonds in a direct trade. A guy who knows how to chamber an AK-47 round doesn't necessarily understand inclusions in diamonds—and has little interest in finding out about them. People being paid off in cash know or think they know what they've got in their hand; most people wouldn't know for certain whether a shiny stone was a diamond or not. They know they don't know, and they prefer not to deal with that problem.

One set of criminals is very much into diamond smuggling, but very few smugglers will ever be handling their hot ice. Jewelry thieves tend to handle their own transportation, from start to finish. They don't trust anyone to handle their stuff, remembering how they came in possession of it to start with. And they have to move their booty somewhere else far away so that a potential buyer is not going to know where the goods came from.

Jewelry thieves use many different methods to acquire their stones, but for the most part the knowledgeable thieves never carry weapons or use violence. When the "hit" is a nonviolent theft crime it is not treated as seriously. Some work like shoplifters. In some cases, a person will distract the clerk while the others clean out jewelry cases. At other times, the thieves follow jewelry salesmen and steal jewels from their cars. Some jewel thieves are expert burglars. A few are simple robbers. People in the last category generally get caught, often while trying to peddle the hot ice elsewhere. The diamond business is a fraternity, and people who use guns on your "brothers" are beyond the pale.

The final major category of smuggler is the "personal use" smuggler. These people almost always take their own risks. A good many of them get caught, too. Personal-use smugglers often buy a stone overseas, then bring it back without declaring it, hoping they can shave a few bucks off their customs bill. Personal-use smuggling is quite common—and often detected. Frankly, personal use smuggling is not worth the hassle if you get caught. For most people it is hardly worth the agitation and worry involved in the process. But some people enjoy it for the rush.

Although the only really legitimate reason to smuggle is found among refugees or people facing draconian currency transfer restrictions, a lot of other people do smuggle diamonds.

"They're so small and pretty, how could you not smuggle them?" I remember that was the gushing comment of a lady who is now very much in trouble with U.S. Customs over one set of smuggled gems that was detected.

Indeed diamonds, which are crystallized carbon, are small and beautiful, and they are valuable.

Diamonds are a concentrated form of wealth, value, or simple sweat—however you want to look at it. *There are no other high-value commodities that are so easily transportable—not to mention concealable—as the gemstone triumvirate: diamonds, rubies, and emeralds.* Thus diamond smuggling is a relatively safe form of smuggling. Gold, platinum, or other high-value metals are heavy, which means they are also relatively bulky.

Cash takes up far more volume and weight than its equivalent value in good-quality diamonds. Cash and precious metals are also more difficult to disguise from the prying eyes of Customs agents than are diamonds.

As much as 15 percent of all existing diamonds have been smuggled at one time or another, which gives some idea of the temptation of diamond smuggling—and how often people succumb to it. The draw is that one or two of the right kind of stones, smuggled and sold, can in fact set you up for life. But even though the possibilities seem endless, the likelihood of making a major windfall from diamond smuggling is really quite different.

Most diamond smugglers make only pocket change. They don't get rich quick; in fact, their work can easily result in major losses. For most smugglers, the profit is money that supplements their day-to-day jobs and supplants the day-to-day drudgery of their lives, injecting an adrenaline rush into a bologna-sandwiches-for-lunch-again pace of living. Yes, many smugglers do it primarily for the excitement, the thrill of beating the odds, the enjoyment of beating "the man."

But in the end, if they keep it up, they all get caught. Sooner or later they make a serious mistake in judgment, or someone gets curious. The game will be over, and arrest and big legal fees can follow.

That's what happened to a particular lady smuggler. She did well, so long as contacts abroad mailed her single, small stones in letters. It was only when she tried a new tactic designed to increase her volume and her profit that she was caught.

PLACES

ANY DIAMOND SMUGGLER HAS TO BE UP TO DATE ON A VARIETY OF ENVIRONMENTS THAT WILL AFFECT HIM. There is the diamond market as a whole, the DeBeers monopoly, and the individual governments involved. The most important key to the diamond market is places to buy and sell and back doors for escape.

Diamond dealing and smuggling starts at the mining centers—the starting point in the diamond market. Diamonds don't grow on trees, and, except for some extremely rare and equally tiny crystals found in meteorites, they don't drop from the sky.

Although "scientists" at different times have claimed that diamonds were formed by everything from lightning strikes to sea creatures, the most recent thinking has it that they are created at about 75 to 120 miles beneath the crust of the earth in certain types of molten rock. They are thrust up from what scientists sometimes call diamond stability fields, by volcanic action. Only here, so far underground that the rocks are plastic, are the temperatures and pressures naturally conducive to carbon atoms forming themselves into the cubic, or isometric, form of crystals that we call diamonds.

How, then, do diamonds go up through dozens of miles of rock and earth? The exact process is not completely known, but it involves what we normally think of as volcanic activity—the molten rock carrying the diamonds oozes upward into and through the earth's crust. This molten diamond-bearing rock solidifies near the surface. It is a little like a spike being driven from the center of the earth toward the surface. The spike of diamond-bearing rock is called a diamond pipe.

Diamond pipes can be mined either by open-pit methods or through tunnels drilled into the pipes, which are generally made of rock known as kimberlite or lamproite. The pipes themselves are known to geologists and diamond hunters as primary deposits.

Surprisingly, kimberlite is not a very tough rock; in fact, wind, rain, sunlight, and other climatic conditions break this diamond-bearing rock down rather quickly. In some parts of the world the diamond pipes—often the cores of mountains—have eroded away. The diamonds that were in those now-eroded pipes have been washed into rivers and streams. Often the stones have been rolled up into sands that are, or were formerly, the ocean shore or bottom. These secondary concentrations along streams, shorelines, and former seabeds are known as alluvial deposits, which may remain in sand and mud (marine deposits), or, in some cases, the sediment may turn into rock. It is alluvial deposits that contain the highest percentage of gem-quality diamonds. There are differing explanations for this, but the most likely one is that badly flawed diamonds are most easily broken and shattered in rivers and streams; the diamonds that survive the natural stone tumbler effect of rivers and ocean tides are generally those that have the fewest imperfections and flaws. Alluvial and marine deposits—because they are concentrations of perhaps whole diamond pipes—generally are extremely rich. There are more carats of diamonds per ton of rock or sand than in diamond pipes.

There is a new theory—one that is of great importance to those prospecting for new diamond sources—that there are other natural conditions that produce diamonds. In Australia's New South Wales there are numerous occurrences of alluvial diamonds, but, contrary to the traditional theory, the area is characterized by a thin, relatively young land crust that has no evidence of kimberlites or lamproites. According to the new theory, diamonds can be formed by the sinking or subduction of carbon-bearing marine sediments in a collision zone between two tectonic plates. If the subducted slab is thick enough, it will remain comparatively cool as it sinks and diamonds will form dynamically during the subduction when sufficiently high pressure is reached. Some calculations show that diamonds could form at depths as shallow as 50 miles, which means that rocks other than kimberlite or lamproite can bring them to the surface. If the theory is correct, it will open new areas to diamond prospecting—and new prospects for diamond dealers and movers.

The theories may be important for some people holding down an academic chair at some university. But for the diamond merchant the realities are the crucial factor. One of those realities is that conditions under which diamonds form are not totally clear. We know that not all volcanic activity produced diamonds. Diamonds are concentrated not only in specific geologic regions—areas where volcanic activity is documented—but in specific geographic areas as well. Although diamonds have been found on every continent except Antarctica, many of the deposits have not proven commercially exploitable.

Theories aside, it appears that diamonds welled up from the depths of the earth as early as 2.5 billion years ago. According to some, the process now seems to have stopped. Natural diamonds are usually not less than 50 million years old. In any event, the stones have been lying there for a long time, just waiting to be picked up in the right place, when the time is right. They've waited a long time.

Diamond mining goes back 3,000 years in India, which was the first home of the diamond industry. It was from those Indian diamond deposits that the stones seeped into Europe and the West—sometimes as pretty baubles, but more often as cultural oddities and rarities. For the most part, the Indian diamond deposits have been effectively depleted through the centuries. Nonetheless, even today India produces some stones and still has an extremely active cutting and polishing industry.

Brazil became a major diamond supplier in the 18th century—a time when people were still debating whether diamonds were formed by lightning. The discovery of alluvial diamond deposits in Brazil brought on a major battle among the early diamond traders.

Indian diamond producers, concerned quite rightly over the effect that the new and rich source was having on their own sales and prices, badmouthed the Brazilian stones. The Indian merchants put out the word that Brazilian diamonds were too difficult to cut. Others denied that there was such a thing as a Brazilian diamond and claimed that the South American stones were just the dregs of Indian stones, brought to Brazil and salted in creeks to create a mining frenzy. The Brazilians struck back at the rumors and the bad publicity by simply shipping their product (smuggling is really more accurate) into India and then selling the diamonds to the public as Indian stones.

But even at this time, the diamond was only a bauble. Perhaps it was an interesting and expensive bauble, but until just a few score years ago, a diamond was a stone prized more for its rarity than any other quality. Frankly, the diamond was dull. It looked dull in nature, and, even when cut and faceted, it looked no better than glass.

In the last half of the 19th century, scientific cutting of diamonds to produce a stone that sparkled and scintillated was unheard of. Most jewelry diamonds were lackluster by today's standards, and certainly diamond engagement bands were not common. Only the very wealthy had diamond jewelry of any kind. The Industrial Revolution was yet to seriously start, and diamonds, a necessary tool of industry today, lacked the significant commercial uses they now have.

At the end of the 19th century, the great South African diamond mines opened up just as the Industrial Revolution swung into high gear. Along came new financial moguls and, in many areas, a middle class that had the economic wherewithal, as well as the incentive, to adorn themselves with jewels.

The South African diamond production eclipsed anything the world had seen. Scientific cutting, to channel the light and reflections inside the stone in precisely calculated ways, made diamonds much more beautiful to behold, and far more attractive to look at and own. The diamond cartel known as DeBeers came into being and promoted diamonds in a way that was unprecedented. The stones became the pinnacle of fashion. That was new! The South African finds and scientific advances combined to create an increased demand at a time when there was a financial ability to satisfy the demand. And any time there is an increased demand there is more of a tendency to smuggle. That tendency remains to this day.

Today, more than 95 percent of all gem diamonds comes from one of five countries—and it is in those places that the dealing and smuggling trail starts.

Australia leads the world, producing more than 30 percent of the world's gem and near-gem diamonds. Actually, Australia accounts for between 35 and 50 percent of the world's total diamond carat output. Australia produces more diamonds by weight than any other country—about three times the annual production of the Commonwealth of Independent States (the vestigial ex-Soviet Union) and four times that of South Africa.

But there are two extremes of value in Australian stones—a very high-grade and a very low-grade diamond. Although Australia's rocky and forbidding terrain has been a source of diamonds since gold miners uncovered the first find in 1851, initially there were low-quality stones overall. That economic disincentive kept a firm lid on the number of exploration companies, and on production, for years.

Later discoveries of diamonds—Australia is also a leader in the production of industrial diamonds—set off a frenzy of exploration that can only be likened to the gold rush that virtually shaped the society and culture of the hard-edged country-continent a century and a half before. Much of the new exploration is taking place in Australia's Northern Territory. But diamonds seem to be everywhere in the outback. The giant Argyle resource in

the Kimberley region of Western Australia, discovered in
1979, is the world's single largest diamond mine, producing 38.9 million carats in 1992. (Only about 10 percent of
its output is rated gem quality.)

There are a lot of other places to look for diamonds.

Botswana—about as easy to find on a map as it is to
get to—weighs in with a hefty 25 percent of the world's
gem diamond production.

Zaire and South Africa—when they're not having
serious domestic economic and political problems that
make diamond smuggling much more interesting to
those who want to leave—each have 12 percent of the
production market. (South African deposits have a high
percentage of gem-quality stones. About 40 percent of
the South African stones fall into that category.) In Zaire
it's said that diamonds are still a dictator's best friend.
The international diamond trade in Zaire, the world's
third largest producer of diamonds of all types, is
believed to be the last remaining major source of hard
currency for the financially pressed government.

The former Soviet Union, specifically the Russian
part, produces about 20 percent of the world's gemstones—but is number two in the production of all rough
(uncut) diamonds. Those grim mines on the permafrost
plains of Siberia are important hard currency earners for
Moscow. Most of the diamonds come from Yakutia, a
region that has given itself semiautonomous status as
the Republic of Sakha. Yakutia in recent years has produced 98 percent of all Russian diamonds.

In Yakutia the signs may say *brilyanty na vsegda*—
diamonds are forever—but here there is little evidence of
the glamour and romance that Madison Avenue pitch-
men and diamond retailers want to attach to the stone.
Russia's diamond miners operate, and have worked for

decades, in some of the world's most disagreeable out-
door working conditions. The remote and forbidding
Siberian outpost is covered in ice nine months a year.
Mush and mud are features the rest of the year.

When Siberian diamonds were discovered in 1949,
the remote and inaccessible region was placed under
Moscow's direct control. Soviet mines first used convict
labor to exploit the resource, with a leavening of volun-
teers from the loyal ranks of the Communist party and
Komsomol (Communist Youth League). As time went by
the government stopped using convicts and relied more
and more on the then-young ideologues, people who saw
diamond production as a means of promoting the party,
their beliefs, and communism. It didn't hurt any that
volunteer diamond workers were always paid better-
than-average wages and allowed extra privileges, such as
avoiding the 10-year waiting list for cars. But the workers' wages were then, and still are, a pittance.

These workers often were "true believers," who
toiled in unspeakable conditions to try to create the
national economic base that was needed to overcome
capitalism. At least that's what they fervently believed
they were doing. The reality was hidden from them.
From 1959 on, they were toiling in the mines so that the
communist leadership of the Soviet Union could market
the fruits of their labor hand in glove with the giant capi-
talist diamond cartel, DeBeers. DeBeers was a pillar of
white South Africa, which was reviled daily in the official Soviet media. But the diamond workers were kept
blissfully ignorant of this connection, which would have
been most troubling to them.

The fall of the Soviet Union not only destroyed the
reason these workers had for working hard—the promo-
tion of their belief in a workers' system where everyone

was supposed to toil according to his or her ability—but it also ripped away their ignorance of the facts. The diamond workers discovered they were toiling in miserable conditions, drawing little pay, so that others (many of them capitalists abroad, including those in South Africa) could profit from their sweat turned to ice. Today Russian workers, particularly older workers in the Russian mines, are unhappy. They want what they see as their due—not only for today's wages, but for their history of misery. For many of today's workers, a purloined stone now means that they can improve their individual lot. These are inventive people who use contacts with the much-feared Russian mafia. But they may also be willing to sell to any high bidder who has hard currency.

The problem is that Yakutia is a nowhere place, a wasteland nobody would visit but for buying diamonds. Because of that, an American, or any foreign traveler who shows up, is immediately pegged for what he is and what he wants, which makes operating clandestinely (or safely) impossible. Only when things change to the extent that it is possible for a foreigner to enter the area without causing a flurry of excitement will diamond deals with local people be possible. That change may be coming soon.

Russia is trying to restructure its diamond market at every level, from the mines to the cutting industry. It badly needs restructuring. Russian managers have made a number of serious miscalculations, including mistakes over when to phase in new mines. The Udachnyi mine, which produces 80 percent of Russia's gems, closes for several months a year due to a buildup of toxic gases at its base. Some Russian mines will soon have to adopt expensive and complicated underground extraction. The opening of the big new Iubileinaya mine, which was scheduled to come on line in 1992, was held up because of delayed deliveries of building materials and supplies.

The newest Russian field is facing many of the same problems that older fields have to deal with. The Lomonosov diamond field is located in Zimnyi Bereg, an area of swampland and taiga forest. There the removal of water, which needs to be done before mining can begin, poses a major technical and ecological problem. But when it gets underway, the field, which comprises five pipes, is likely to become extremely profitable because half the diamonds are of very high quality. About half of the stones are gem quality, and many of the rest are near gem.

Despite the grim realities and serious mistakes in the Russian fields, there is a lot of "happy talk" among Russian diamond experts. Talk to the market leaders in the Siberian diamond industry and they will tell you that sooner or later one of the main diamond markets in the world will be in Russia. The diamond bosses of Siberia say they will soon have a secondary market in diamonds and, eventually, 10 or 15 polishing plants in the Yakutia region. That would have repercussions for diamond merchants and smugglers if it comes about.

Given diamonds' economic importance to Russia, both the nation's parliament and its president keep a close watch on the diamond industry and those in it. A state company has the Russian monopoly in mining, sorting, and grading rough diamonds from Yakutia. And the Almazyuvelier export firm handles diamond export sales.

It's probably true that Russian diamond fields are now being tapped better than in previous years; under more normal circumstances that should produce a drop in smuggling. But given the political, economic, and social turmoil there today, and the greater turmoil that is on the horizon for Russia during the rest of the 1990s and the first years of the new millennium, illicit diamond dealing and smuggling will continue to be a growing business in Russia. In fact, smuggling of all kinds is a multibillion-dollar business in the former Soviet Union.

Smuggling, in any form, is not likely to go away in the vast reaches of Russia and will continue to plague the Russian government and economy. In just a few years, smuggling has become too rooted in the society to be stopped easily. The practice of accepting bribes in return for assisting in what are euphemistically called "illegal exports" has become almost commonplace in government-owned enterprises, the Customs service, and government offices. For instance, the standard bribe to a rank-and-file Customs officer to look the other way is $20. That's not much by American standards, but there that $20 is the equivalent of two months of official salary. That's a temptation that is hard not to give in to. Even the armed forces appear to be involved in smuggling, and there are some indications that secret military airfields are increasingly being used as bases for such operations.

A decade ago there was an Iron Curtain. Today Russia has what can best be called a porous border. The readjustment of national borders after the Soviet Union split into more than a dozen independent states in 1991 created for Russia, and the other new nations, untold thousands of miles of new national boundaries.

Lines that formerly marked only administrative areas suddenly became national frontiers. Those threads of administrative lines became a skein of long, unprotected national borders, many without fences or border posts that now run between Russia, the Baltic states, Ukraine, and Belarus and that are open or nearly so.

Long, open borders figure in every smuggler's most pleasant dreams.

Significant amounts of smuggling—some would call it illegal trade in raw materials—already go through the Baltic nations of Estonia, Latvia, and Lithuania. Those are countries where the people remain almost genetically friendly to Americans because of U.S. support of the "captive nations" through decades of Soviet domination. The Baltic states, which have traditionally served as Russia's window to the West, have become Russia's open door to the West, and all kinds of things pass through that door now.

Any American diamond pipeline out of Russia is probably going through very friendly territory if it runs through the Baltic states. Not only do the people there like Americans, but they despise the Russians. Baltic police officers have every reason to be sullen when dealing with their Russian law enforcement counterparts, who, until only a few years ago, were their oppressors. Law enforcement agencies in the Baltic states may provide some help to the Russians in a murder case; however, Baltic police generally find something better to do when the Russian police ask for help in investigating "economic crimes," such as diamond smuggling.

Not all the potential smuggling areas are as far away as the swamps of Russia. Soon to come on line as a major player in the diamond world will be Canada.

An area of Canada that was once windswept wilderness, best left to wolves, martens, and bears, has now been dubbed the Corridor of Hope. The frenzied winds of exploration swept the tundra around Lac de Gras after diamonds were discovered there in 1991. At one point, more than 200 firms were probing for kimberlite pipes in the tundra. The Canadian finds promise to rival any in

Russia and, eventually, Australia. In fact it is an Australian mining giant, Broken Hill Pty. Co., Ltd., that teamed with the Canadian exploration firm, Dia Met Minerals, Ltd., and set out to develop the Lac de Gras diamond deposit, which some say is one of the world's richest untapped sources. Major international mining concerns, including South Africa's giant DeBeers Consolidated Mines, Ltd., quickly joined the Canadian carbon rush. (Stock share prices of Canadian exploration ventures soared in a messy, and predictable, run-up of stock prices. But the stock bubble burst after several highly touted ventures announced dismal test results.)

Despite the bust stock market activity, the Canadian prospects are real. Canada remains, in fact, a diamond in the rough. At least some of the large-scale tests have shown that the properties there have extremely rich kimberlite pipes, which are not much different from the kimberlite pipes in diamond-rich South Africa and Russia, where mining has been successful. But the key to keep in mind is that all the mines in those locations took more than a decade to develop fully. Additionally, the timing of any Canadian development will likely be slowed somewhat by environmentalists. As in Russia, much of the Canadian mining would involve draining lakes since the diamond deposits are located under lake beds. Any mining means there will be massive environmental changes, so it's no surprise that environmental activists are gearing up to fight the first major diamond mine on the continent. But despite the environmentalists' best efforts, diamond production could begin before the dawn of the new millennium. All of this activity points to potential diamond-smuggling operations.

Other diamond-producing countries include

Namibia, Brazil, Central African Republic, and Angola. There is also some production in Sierra Leone, Tanzania, China, Guinea, Liberia, Ghana, Venezuela, Swaziland, India, Indonesia, Ivory Coast, and Guyana.

Lesotho, which had a diamond rush of its own in the late 1960s, is relatively overlooked and underworked today. There is a potential for better recovery in the future. Given its geographic isolation, the opportunities for smuggling are good there.

Angola actually deserves a few more words than a simple listing as an also-ran. Angolan diamonds have been a major factor on the world market, although unofficially. The Angolan diamond history is a good example of what can happen when the fire of revolt and war meets "hot ice"—diamonds that are illegally mined or are smuggled. It gives some insight into the complex, confusing world of diamond politics and economics and is a window into DeBeers, the mother of all monopolies.

For years, the Angolan government and a rebel force known as UNITA battled for supremacy in Angola. Political instability in the country allowed wildcat diggers, or *garimpeiros*, to plunder alluvial diamond beds in Angola's Cuango province. It has been estimated that in some years more than 10 percent of the world's total diamond output came from this single source.

Some of the money from free-lancers' efforts went into miners' pockets, of course. Much of it was apparently siphoned off to provide arms for UNITA, which had the backing of the apartheid South African government.

The DeBeers monopoly, which tries to capture every smuggled or illegally mined diamond and process the stone through its subsidiary Central Selling Organization (CSO), was naturally interested in recapturing the illicit Angolan production. At the very least, the production posed a threat, as does any outside source, to the monopoly.

But there were some interesting sidelights. Some insisted that the close connection of DeBeers to the South African government, and of the South African government to UNITA, amounted to an unlovely triangle. There were even claims that CSO was paying way over the going diamond price to the wildcat miners, a gift to UNITA, but this was a claim that DeBeers's people have always denied.

What is important is that the control of the Angolan diamond fields became very important to military campaigns. Whoever lost control of the taxing/expropriation abilities also lost a major source of revenue. That lesson has ramifications in every country, under any regime, where diamonds are produced.

One area that should be considered for the future may well be Zambia. It doesn't presently have a diamond mining industry to speak of; most of its stones are actually smuggled in from neighboring countries. However, there is a great potential for Zambia to produce diamonds since its geology is similar to neighboring diamond producers Zaire and Angola.

There are reportedly diamonds in the hills of central Vietnam, and that could be another area with an as yet unrealized potential.

What many people find interesting about the list of diamond-producing countries is that, except for Australia and Canada, just about every location listed is facing serious internal strife. That sort of political/social condition makes illicit diamond mining and smuggling much more attractive to people living in such places. In some cases, diamond smuggling is literally their ticket out—a virtual lifeline.

There are no such "instability" incentives in the case of Canada. But for Americans Canada is a northern neighbor. And for the would-be diamond smuggler there are some positive aspects. Canada has what amounts to an open border with the United States. The two nations share a common language, as well as a culture that a potential illicit diamond buyer or smuggler can operate in without feeling—or seeming—out of place.

Except for Australia and Canada, the very places that produce diamonds seem generally less able to defend against smugglers. "Look-the-other-way-for-a-price" officials and the prevalence of people who have strong incentives to get often illegally obtained stones out of the country make a smuggler's life easier. Yet in any locale, unless the would-be smuggler knows the territory like the back of his hand, has the right contacts, and can lay his hands on the right stones without having to ask around, there are going to be big problems.

Because uncut diamonds have yet to be made into jewels, they are relatively cheap at the diamond-mining stage of the process. And they are relatively cheap for the would-be smuggler to buy.

But when you buy an uncut diamond—assuming for the moment that you do really get a diamond—there is often no way for anyone except a professional to know with absolute certainty whether it is gem quality. Even if it is gem quality, how large will the finished stone be? The answer to that is crucial. Remember, carat weight of the finished stone, not the rough diamond, is one of the four keys to the value of the diamond. Two or three carats of tiny stones are not worth anything near what a single stone of two or three carats can bring. That should be enough to discourage most thinking novices from getting into the diamond-dealing business at the level of dealing in uncut diamond, or *rough.*

And although smuggling something like a diamond out of a Third- or Fourth-World diamond-producing country may seem like a breeze, it isn't all that easy. Many little countries aren't keen on having diamonds exported illegally. Why? Because top officials—oops, make that the government leaders—always manage to find some nice way to take a cut of the Customs proceeds. Since a smuggled diamond usually doesn't put anything in their pockets, they're more than a little miffed. It's like stealing from *them!* In such countries you may soon have a bigger problem than getting a stone out of the country—how to get yourself out of jail. In many of these backwater nations, the mere suspicion of smuggling, rather than actual proof, is usually sufficient evidence for the gendarmerie to make an arrest and for a judge to pass sentence.

Even if you don't end up in some jail that makes the Black Hole of Calcutta look like a five-star hotel, it's likely you'll be taken for a greenhorn—and a pile of American greenbacks—if you start out dealing in rough diamonds.

Most professional jewelers who deal in diamonds daily can't tell by looking whether some object put in front of them is an uncut or rough diamond. Most of them have never seen a diamond in the rough; many have never even seen a picture of one. That thing in front of them could look like what they think is a rough diamond, but it might actually be the bottom of a Coke bottle, skillfully cleaved and covered with a thin coat of oil or petroleum jelly (many rough diamonds are slightly oily). Diamonds in their uncut and unpolished form seldom look anything like the diamonds most people know.

More than one would-be diamond entrepreneur has found out, to his dismay, that the uncut bargain-basement "stone" came not from a secret diamond deposit but from the bottom of a no-deposit, no-return bottle.

For the would-be free-lance diamond dealer or gem runner, there are some pluses—but a whole lot more disadvantages—when dealing anywhere in the miner-to-cutter levels.

From the mining centers, diamonds go to the cutting centers. Usually, the stones are still under DeBeers's control as they start this part of the process. It is from the cutting centers to the distributors that a good part of the commercial diamond smuggling emanates.

For the most part, smart smugglers operate on the interfaces. The first interface, of course, is at the mining centers, where the stones start their journey into the world of commerce. The second interface is where uncut diamonds become finished stones that are suitable for jewelry. The second interface is the point where jewelry-quality diamonds move from cutter to seller. (There are exceptions, of course. Some smugglers move only industrial-grade diamonds to people who have a big need and relatively little money, for instance.)

Again, the *where* of the interfaces is an important issue for the diamond smuggler. Cutting centers and selling centers are a Mecca for smugglers of both rough and finished stones—sellers trying to dispose of rough and buyers planning to take diamonds elsewhere.

Diamond cutting is a high-value industry that operates on fine margins, something that diamond buyers need to be aware of when they're dickering over prices.

Antwerp, Belgium, is often touted as the world's principal diamond-cutting center. Many consider India the largest seller of polished diamonds in the world because about 2,000 merchants are involved in the business. Indian cutters tend to be highly competitive in their pricing structure, though many in the business sniff at much of the work that comes out of there. The common comment is that "you get what you pay for."

Israel is also a key cutting and polishing center. There are also new polishing centers like Thailand, Sri Lanka, and Malaysia.

Historically, the major markets for polished diamonds have been the United States, Europe, and Japan. But the past is not always prologue.

The medium-term outlook for retail sales is the key factor in where diamond dealing—and smuggling—will be lucrative. At present, the experts seem to agree that there will probably be an upsurge in demand in Southeast Asia, including Thailand, Taiwan, and China. Retail sales should be lower in Japan, but they will probably be higher in the United States. Europe will continue to buy, but the overall European economy has been an anchor on sales. Sales in France and Germany have tapered off, though the purchasing impulse is still strong in Italy. Although Russia has not been a major market in more than seven decades, the internal demand in Russia is growing greater as a free-market economy comes into being. Nouveau riche Russians love the sparkling stones for their beauty; even the Russian men adore them as a status symbol. Russia cannot be overlooked as a major market, as well as a source in the future. But it will be open only to people who have the correct connections.

3

DeBeers

In the diamond business, even today, the sun never sets on DeBeers. An economic empire unto itself, the DeBeers cartel—call it a monopoly and you won't be far from wrong—is both loved and hated by most of the people in the diamond business. It has subsidiaries to deal with, and dominate, virtually all phases of the market.

DeBeers has corporate ownership links with DeBeers Consolidated Mines Ltd., a South African corporation known for its control of the natural diamond industry. The London-based Diamond Trading Corporation (DTC) is a DeBeers tentacle that controls much of the world's diamond trade.

The Central Selling Organization (CSO), which operates in England, South Africa, and Switzerland, was created by DeBeers in the Great Depression of the 1930s, when there was little demand for such luxuries as diamonds. Ask DeBeers representatives and, if they deigned to answer you, they would say the cartel signs contracts with producers so that it can guarantee steady sales and prices. But these contracts also impose quotas on the producers. Take the spin doctors out of the picture, and it's fair to say that DeBeers's selling organization intentionally limits supplies to maintain price stability.

DeBeers subsidiaries sell diamonds to about 160 customers, most of them cutters, polishers, and dealers in the main cutting centers in Belgium, Israel, the United States, and India. DeBeers controls prices by selling at sights, which are take-it-or-leave-it sessions where DeBeers invites a select group of diamond buyers and offers each individual customer a parcel of diamonds that it has decided would be best for the particular buyer. (These parcels of uncut rough are also called sights.) Generally, there are good stones and bad stones in each parcel, or sight, and buyers don't get to sift through to choose the ones they want. Up or down, yea or nay, da or nyet. Any way you say it, there are only two possible choices. The selected diamond merchants seldom turn down the rough stones they are offered; they would have a hard time getting any elsewhere, so effective is DeBeers at vacuuming up all the world's rough. And if they rejected too many parcels, they would no longer be invited to the sights. When DeBeers says, "Take 'em or leave 'em," most people take them.

By regulating the supply and stockpiling surpluses, the cartel is able to flatten the fluctuations that are natural to any commodity market. It has a noble sound to it. DeBeers's former chairman, Harry Oppenheimer, was once quoted as saying, "Whether this measure of control amounts to a monopoly I would not know, but if it does, it is certainly a monopoly of a most unusual kind. There is no one concerned with diamonds, whether as producer, dealer, cutter, jeweler, or customer, who does not benefit from it."

That's not the way that everyone sees the situation.

DeBeers is capable of economically blackjacking any-body who crosses the cartel. The reality is that because DeBeers has a monopoly position and is run by good businessmen, it acts on the understanding of the impor-tance of keeping prices up.

DeBeers is certainly no friend of the consumer. DeBeers is also no friend of the free-lance diamond smuggler who is moving any kind of goods that could compete with its own. DeBeers has a reputation that makes smuggling of rough . . . well, rough.

Whether you like them or not, the practices of DeBeers and its subsidiaries, rapacious as they are, create and dominate the atmosphere that diamond dealers and smugglers work in. Even independent diamond mer-chants can buy in the bush of Angola or in a shop in Antwerp and be certain that when they turn over the stone later, the "value" will not have been eroded by the sudden discovery of some rich new source that will dilute the value of the present stocks.

With DeBeers at the helm of the diamond business, even a rich new source of diamonds will release its stones into the market in an orderly, undeflationary way. At the same time, the type of price stability enforced by DeBeers means that diamond cutters and dealers aren't going to get any cut rates for large orders; there is no pref-erential treatment for buying in volume. Unlike an auto manufacturer, DeBeers has no "fleet sales" prices. That does mean there is some economic incentive for smug-gling, provided that the smuggling somehow cuts the cost of doing business for the diamond merchant—and provided the smuggler can get the stones past Customs agents and DeBeers's agents.

DeBeers, despite its size and historical stranglehold on the market, is riding out rough times. And the times have been getting progressively worse. The rough-diamond market is a $4-to-$5-billion-a-year business. DeBeers controls about 80 percent, four-fifths, of the world's rough diamond market through its London-based CSO. About half of CSO diamonds go for industrial uses, while 12 to 14 percent end up as jewelry. However, in terms of value, the jewelry market accounts for some 80 to 90 percent of the worth of sales. The Diamond Trading Co., Ltd., is the gem-diamond-marketing arm of DeBeers. This corporate entity buys stones from another DeBeers arm, the Diamond Purchasing and Trading Co., Ltd., in the convoluted web of interlocking companies.

A key to the future of the whole operation is the CSO stone reserves. CSO maintains a stockpile of diamonds that was believed to have jumped by $400 million to $4.12 billion at the end of 1993, from $3.76 billion in 1992. While the figures are estimates at best, they do give an order of magnitude of DeBeers's investment in the future of diamonds. If production stopped at every diamond mine in the world, there would be no effect on supply for nearly a year. That's a passel of inventory and economic power.

An inventory of the magnitude and a position of such power is seldom matched, but it is important for the diamond merchant of the future to understand that there is growing pressure from Russia and other producers on DeBeers's CSO. In the 1990s, DeBeers is battling an oversupplied market and a relatively sluggish demand. Japan has cut CSO diamond imports in dollar terms. Russia has admitted to having its own stockpile of high-quality gems worth at least $3 billion (more honest estimates suggest $5 billion is more likely), much of which is apparently finding its way onto the market outside CSO. That Russian stockpile poses a potential threat to DeBeers—in fact, the Russian diamond organization has the potential to go head to head with DeBeers. The Russians are about the only ones who could get into an "ice war" and beat DeBeers.

Nonetheless, Russia is considered unlikely to sell its sizable stockpile of diamonds; "dumping" diamonds would destroy the confidence of both the diamond trade and of diamond purchasers of all types. Dumping stones would also devalue the remaining Russian stockpiles.

Even though the situation seems to be sorting itself out, and Russia gives signs of falling into line with DeBeers, it is expected to take three to five years for demand to catch up with supply. Cutters, polishers, and retailers are failing to restock diamonds as they make sales, a move that probably reflects a lack of confidence that the world economy will rebound. While DeBeers expresses continued confidence that worldwide retail sales are holding fairly steady, the fact is that retailers have been letting their stocks dwindle. Retailers may sell five pieces today, yet reorder one or two instead of five. That means that at present there is less need for stones, no matter how they get from miner to merchant.

How the situation will sort itself out in the early 21st century remains to be seen. But don't bet against DeBeers.

A DIAMOND MOVER'S HAND-BOOK

CHAPTER

DIAMONDS—THE BASIC PRODUCT

DIAMONDS ARE A FORM OF CARBON THAT CRYSTALLIZES IN ONE CERTAIN WAY—WHAT GEM FANCIERS CALL AN ISOMETRIC ARRANGEMENT. There are subgroupings of the isometric arrangement, and all are diamonds, all are valuable. The isometric arrangement means the crystals tend to be balanced in all directions. This crystal arrangement is called cubic. But other forms of carbon crystals, other than those in the isometric arrangement, are virtually valueless. They're used for lubricating locks. Graphite, the black stuff of lead pencils, is essentially pure carbon, but it crystallizes in a different structure.

The typical gem diamond is 99.95-percent-plus pure carbon. That tiny remainder can be made up of more than a score of different impurity elements. Sometimes these elements can influence the color or the shape of the stone.

Diamonds are generally measured in the following four key categories:

• Color

- Cut
- Clarity
- Carat weight

As important as the Four Cs are, the ludicrous part is that they are only a measure of value. They do not measure the beauty of a stone. For instance, a small stone may be more beautiful than a larger one a color grade lower—but it will not be as valuable. And value, not beauty, is what the diamond smuggling business is all about.

The standards applied to diamonds are more stringent than those used in almost any other consumer product line. Minute differences in color or weight—differences that can be seen only under 10X magnification—make for huge differences in price. The simple fact is that the value of any diamond is based strictly on rarity. Beauty—and it's hard to stress this too much—seldom has anything to do with the value. Again, it's the Four Cs: color, cut, clarity, and carat weight.

If you haven't memorized that litany by now, stop right here and don't resume reading until you've done so. You can forget your significant other's name or birthday; you can't afford to forget those words if you're in the diamond business.

These are the key determinants of diamond rarity, the standards by which all fashioned diamonds are judged, paid for, and sold. Anyone who doesn't understand these factors is going to be hornswoggled—sooner rather than later, undoubtedly.

When you're haggling over the price of stones you have got to be able to accurately assess the color, cut, clarity, and weight to make your own appraisal of the value. When dealing with stones that have not been traveling—or will not be traveling—through the convention-al channels, it's particularly important that you be able to articulate why the price should be based on your appraisal and not on the other person's idea of the price.

You need to display superior knowledge—knowledge that is so readily apparent to your counterpart that he is willing to agree to your price. In the real world that may not happen, even if you are 100-percent correct. A seller may feel certain he can peddle his diamonds to some other, less knowledgeable buyer for more money than he can get from you. A potential buyer may be impressed with your knowledge of stones but still figure he can get comparable quality at a lower price from one of your competitors who is less well versed on the trade. But you cannot afford to be thought of as a neophyte; you have to acquire knowledge, experience, and a whole new vocabulary.

The weight of a stone is the first thing most people think of when their minds wander to diamonds. It's as good a place as any for you to start your journey into the diamond field.

CARAT WEIGHT

Weight is an important factor in determining value, whether the diamond is rough (uncut) or finished (e.g., cut, polished).

Remember that diamond price is based on rarity. Since there are fewer large stones, the value of a stone increases exponentially per carat. The price of a four-carat piece of rough diamond (assuming all other aspects of the stone are equal) will be much more than the price a cutter would pay for four one-carat pieces of rough, for instance. And the price of a finished one-carat stone wouldn't be anywhere near close to a quarter of what a four-carat stone of the same color, cut, and clarity would bring.

Diamond weights, and the weight of other gems as well, are expressed in the metric carat. This equals 0.200 grams, a little more than 0.007 ounce. This is a minuscule weight.

How tiny? Keep in mind that most of the general public seems to think that a diamond engagement ring has to have a one-carat stone (very few do) or it really isn't a ring worth mentioning. Let's play with that popular misconception for a minute, while keeping in mind that a one-carat diamond may retail from the low thousands to the ten-thousand-dollar range, depending on color and other factors. A diamond dealer could use a single first-class postage stamp to mail the stones for 141 one-carat-diamond rings, and there would still be some weight left over. To put it another way: if you wanted to mail diamonds you could send more than 141 carats of stones before you would need a second stamp! That's how small the carat weight measurement is.

But the people in the diamond trade don't conduct their business on a weight so gross as the carat. Of course not. Farmers may sell their crops by the ton, but you don't buy heads of lettuce, bunches of carrots, or steaks by the ton. You buy food by the pound—a small portion of the ton.

The same holds true with diamond dealers. They routinely measure the weight of their stones to 1/1,000th of a carat, and they price the stone in rounded-off 1/100ths of a carat—called *points*.

This is another of the diamond terms that must be fully understood. Although some diamond jewelry may have individual stones weighing a point or two, and there are pieces of jewelry where the main stone weighs in excess of 100 points or one carat, the vast majority of jewelry stones are between five points and one carat—the area where everyone talks about points. For that reason *point* becomes one of the most important words in a diamond dealer's lexicon.

And it takes a lot of understanding. Admittedly, learning the jargon of the diamond trade is just about as easy as learning English or Japanese. If you're brought up with it, it's natural. If not, it's hard to acquire. But again, you've got to acquire the language and be able to use it effortlessly and flawlessly. Anything else will identify you as a tenderfoot in the diamond business.

Let's take an example of the difficulties of expressing weight measurements: a stone that weighs between a half and a two-thirds of a carat (.63 carat). Diamond dealers don't say "point sixty-three carats." They will say it weighs "63 points" or call it a "63-pointer." Let's take another stone, one of about half a carat, say .45 point. It is called a 45-pointer or is said to weigh 45 points.

Seems simple enough.

Now let's go to a stone that weighs more than one carat, for instance, a stone of 1.08 carats. The pros will say the stone weighs "one point oh eight carats" or is "one oh eight." "Point" in the first case is used to identify the decimal mark; in the second example the word is dropped completely. In the diamond trade you can't afford to make a mistake when talking about diamonds. You've got to be carefully taught. The use of point, like that of the Four Cs, has to become reflexive.

There is one other word that the diamond dealer has to know and know how to use. The word is spelled *melee* but it rhymes with *belly*. Melee is a generic term that refers to small diamonds, diamonds under 20 or 25 points.

If you understand everything up to now and can talk intelligently about weight, now is the time to go on so that you can really get confused. But *do not* go on, even to the period at the end of this sentence, if you haven't mastered the language above.

When the weight of a finished diamond is under a carat, there are several ways of referring to the stone. We have talked about one way already, referring to the diamond weight by the number of points—25 points, 87 points, etc. That's the most accurate way. But there are a lot of other terms that are thrown around in the trade, and you'll need to know them if you want to pass as knowledgeable in the business. Often people in the trade will refer to stones as fractions, but don't think that a "half" is necessarily 50 points or a "quarter" 25 points.

In this nomenclature a half could be anywhere from 47 through 56 points. Although usage may vary slightly, a point or two in some cases, people using this fraction system generally mean the following:

Term	Range of Weight
1/10	.09-.11 carat
1/8	.12-.14 carat
1/6	.15-.17 carat
1/5	.18-.22 carat
1/4	.23-.29 carat
1/3	.30-.37 carat
3/8	.38-.46 carat
1/2	.47-.56 carat
5/8	.57-.69 carat
3/4	.70-.83 carat
7/8	.84-.89 carat
9/10	.90-.95 carat

Let's throw in another system. You can't blink an eye or frown when the person you deal with starts talking about *grainers*. Diamond wholesalers—people you may well have to deal with at one end or the other of a transaction—have their own language that is based on the pearl grain weight—one-fourth of a carat. Thus a .75-carat stone would be a *three grainer*, but so would a .68-carat stone or an .83-carat stone. Such usage is an approximation at best, but one you'll need to know and feel comfortable with.

In another measurement system, stones are referred to by the number that it takes to make a carat. Tenth-of-a-carat stones, for instance, would be called tens; tiny .005-carat diamonds would be two hundreds. Often this system is used for recording information on invoices. When it is used that way the figure is recorded like a fraction.

Size in Carats	Oral	Written
.005	Two hundreds	1/200
.007	One fifties	1/150
.008	One twenty-fives	1/125
.01	Hundreds	1/100
.015	Seventies	1/70
.02	Fifties	1/50
.03	Thirty-threes	1/33
.10	Tens	1/10
.125	Eights	1/8

When diamonds are over a carat, they are defined in terms of the carat weight to the nearest 100th of a carat—"two point oh three carats," is the way a stone of 2.03 carats would be described.

The weight of a diamond is in most ways the most objective of all the Four Cs. Loose diamonds can be weighed on a jeweler's scale, or balance, as it is often called, and the weight of mounted stones can be estimated. (Mounted diamonds cannot be weighed; they must first be unmounted. Even though it is possible to measure a mounted stone and then apply a complex set of formulas to the measurements to get a reasonably approximate weight, people involved in the movement of diamonds across borders should seldom do so. That's being generous. Offhand, there are no good reasons I can think of to ever use only weight approximations of mounted stones in making purchases. If you're really serious about buying stones set in jewelry, unmount the stones and weigh them before buying. As will become apparent later, there are too many people out to swindle you, in too many ways, with already mounted goods.)

For examining, weighing, and measuring diamonds, you will need some special equipment.

You will constantly need to look at diamonds under magnification. A 10X color-corrected loupe—either a hand-held one or one that fits in the eye/clips on the glasses—is the standard of the diamond industry. Most users of loupes quickly find that hand-held ones, ones that look like small magnifying glasses, are not as versatile as the kind held up against the eye or clipped to glasses. The reason is simple: often you will want to use both hands in examining a diamond; hand-held loupes make that impossible.

The most common weighing devices in the smuggling trade are diamond balances. Some are so small they can be carried in a (thick) wallet. The hand-held ones are simple to use and operate. Place the stone in one pan, then add the tiny weights to the other pan with a tweezers until the pans balance. Add up the total of the weights. There's nothing difficult about it if you can add.

A good portable balance will allow you to measure the weight of a diamond to within one-half point.

At times you'll need to measure the dimensions of stones. In the diamond trade, the stones are measured to the nearest 100th of a millimeter—a distance of about four 10,000ths of an inch, or, more precisely .0003937 of an inch.

For measurements, your best bet is a screw micrometer. Some people use other devices called moe gauges and leveridge gauges with success (and an eye on the instruction book), but I prefer a micrometer. Micrometers are readily available almost anywhere, including hardware stores. In the United States, most micrometers are designed to measure in inches rather than millimeters, which is what you'll need in the diamond business. You could take the measurement in inches and then use a conversion formula. But why? Save yourself a lot of hassle, and perhaps some expensive mistakes, by buying a micrometer that measures in millimeters from the very start.

Hole gauges—thin sheets of metal or plastic with holes punched out in a variety of common diamond sizes—are also helpful if you don't need accuracy.

Any of this equipment can be purchased at jewelry supply firms.

By the way, when you buy equipment like this, don't leave tell-tale tracks behind you. Don't buy locally. Pay cash. Don't put the purchases on a credit card, and don't give your correct name or address. Generally, using a friend's name and address is sufficient, and you won't stumble over it as so many people do when they start using made up names or phony addresses and phone numbers. And don't keep the receipts. You probably won't need them for tax purposes!

COLOR

Color has several meanings in the diamond world. Usually the most sought-after diamonds are colorless—a trait that is so desirable, so rare, and so often misused as a sales pitch that the U.S. Federal Trade Commission (FTC) had to come up with a set of regulations to define what colorless really is.

The reality is that very few diamonds—professionals refer to them as stones, and you should do so from now on—are colorless. Diamonds come in a wide variety of colors; the colors are the result of minor distortions in the crystal structure, natural impurities, or radiation and heat treatment. In nature most stones are slightly shaded either toward the brown or the yellow. Most stones sold to consumers run the gamut from near-colorless to slightly yellow or brown. Diamonds do come in virtually all other colors, however, including blue, pink, gray, and orange.

Because of their rarity, colorless stones are very valuable, assuming that the cut, clarity, and carat weight are reasonably good. As traces of color can be seen—first under magnification and then with the naked eye—the stones progressively lose value. Up to a point! When the color in a stone is so intense that it is readily apparent to the naked eye, the stones start gaining in value again from the color. Then their value increases as the color deepens. Fancy colors are evaluated on the basis of tone and saturation. Such fancy-color diamonds are desirable, particularly when the color is natural.

But not all coloring in diamonds is natural. Diamond colors can be changed, and most of the colors found in nature can be reproduced by technicians working with normal color-grade diamonds. Blues, purples, greens, and pinks are fairly rare among the treated stone colors, but it is much easier to create fancy yellows, browns (called coffees), oranges, and yellow- or blue-greens.

Irradiation, or irradiation and heat treatment, will produce some color changes. These are so-called treated stones. Properly irradiated diamonds, those that have been done in modern times, are completely safe for the wearer or bearer. However, some stones treated in the early 1900s are themselves radioactive and unsuitable for wearing.

Colors can also be changed or "improved" by skullduggery with the object of increasing the price. Mounting stones with colored foil backings or placing dots of paint, fingernail polish, or ink at certain places on the stone are some of the easier ways to do it—and easier to detect. But real pros use ultrathin coatings of chemicals or plastics to defraud buyers—but those materials can be so ingeniously applied that they can't be detected outside a professional gemology laboratory. For that reason, colored diamonds are a good thing to stay away from in the smuggling trade unless you carry a fully equipped lab with you.

The amount of color that is visible in any diamond depends on several factors. The larger the stone, the more the color will be noticed. The method of cutting will have some effect on color. The pointed ends of fancy shapes such as pears, hearts, and marquise-shaped diamonds are generally more colorful; diamond professionals have a saying that the points of the stones "draw color."

Particularly in colored stones, stay away from those already in mounts. A good jeweler can use the color of the metal mounting to improve the look of a stone. In certain mountings slightly yellow or brown diamonds seem to be more colorless, while in other mountings dark yellows and browns seem richer and darker. Blue-tinged stones are enhanced by silver mountings. Conversely, white metal usually does very little good for yellow or brown stones. Gold-colored mountings are bad for bluish stones; they deaden the color.

Hold it. All this talk about color—does that mean that someone who is color blind cannot work in the diamond business effectively? No. The need to see colors as we normally understand it is one of the many myths in the diamond-dealing profession. Except when dealing with fancy-colored stones, color-blind people do well— sometimes exceptionally well—as color graders. They are not judging the hue of a color, but rather the depth of the color, and it makes no difference to them whether the hue is yellow, green, or brown.

There are a lot of other myths that the jewelry trade has built up about color, and it's worthwhile to explore them here because they affect the business of buying and selling diamonds.

The biggest myth is that you have to have a colorless stone or you've just got junk. People outside the trade, even when you try to show them the distinction between the color of the top five color grades on mounted stones, just can't tell any difference. To the viewer there is no discernible difference. These top color grades simply measure relative rarity—and thus are a way of measuring price. Such finely tuned color grades turn out to be distinctions made by professionals, but there is no difference in the eye of the ultimate diamond purchaser. Of course, when you're going to be dealing with those diamond middlemen in buying or selling, you've got to honor the myth. They do. And you need to be reading from the same page in the book.

A similar myth is that, within the normal color ranges, people want the more colorless stone. In fact, when you put unmounted stones out, many people will choose stones from the darker end of a normal range. Ask them why and they will tell you they seem "richer" or "warmer" than the colorless ones.

But it's unlikely that you'll be dealing with customers in a jewelry store. You're going to be dealing with a merchant or some other middleman. So, the myths aside, when you're dealing with stones to sell to others, the less color the better.

Color has been called "the subtle C," because the gradations are so slight that they are virtually indistinguishable except to a trained professional who has master stones to grade against, using a 10X loupe.

The importance of owning a set of master stones for color grading cannot be overstated. People who think that they can "hold color" in their memories—and there are many so-called professionals who profess to be able to do this—are looking for trouble and financial losses. Few people can consistently match paint, carpeting, or sewing material without taking along a color swatch for comparison. When dealing in the thousands and tens of thousands of dollars rather than $19.95-a-square-yard carpet, the diamond dealer needs his own color swatches, or master stones.

Full sets of master stones run to dozens of diamonds. But most dealers need only a few to mark key points in their own business—as few as five, or sometimes even three, often will suffice for field grading.

Master stones are diamonds that have been carefully graded for color only. They mark dividing lines between different color grades. When comparing a master stone with the stone being graded, it is comparatively easy to say "that stone has more color" or "that stone has less color" than the master stone. The grader then uses a second master stone, one that marks another dividing line, to see if the stone has more or less color. By getting the stone between two successive dividing lines on whatever color scale is being used, the diamond dealer can grade the stone as to color—an essential step in determining value.

While the use of master stones is important, it is also important to keep close track of them. These diamonds are easy to mix up with the stone or stones being graded—and difficult to locate once again. And no, you do not put a drop of red fingernail polish on them to aid identification. That destroys their value as master stones for color grading.

The causes of color in diamonds vary and are really unimportant to most diamond merchants. It is probably enough to understand that brown and red (really pink) colors in diamonds are due to a distortion of the crystal structure. Green seems to be associated with changes in the structure of the diamond crystal resulting from radiation (natural or man-induced). Blue diamonds result from nearly infinitesimal amounts of boron impurities being mixed into the crystal structure. Blue-violet colors in diamonds are apparently linked to traces of nitrogen. Other colors seem to be linked to a combination of structural distortions and chemical impurities.

When grading, a diamond dealer has to understand that when stones are of the same color grade, sometimes the actual color, whether brown or yellow, makes a difference. It is generally easier for people to pick out the tinges of yellow than it is for them to see browns. For that reason, when grading browns you must use extra care in determining exactly what you have—and how much you should pay for it.

As mentioned before—and don't forget it—among the fancy colors the browns and yellows are the most common. Going up the rarity scale are gray diamonds, pink ones, and blue ones. In the *very rare* category you'll find oranges, greens, and purples/violets. Red diamonds are almost nonexistent; they're usually a dark pink at best.

It's important for anyone who plans on dealing in diamonds to know the market when it comes to color and color grades. Light yellows and light browns sell well in many parts of the United States; bringing those into the country is a wise business proposition. But Far Eastern buyers want colorless, pink, or blue stones; bringing a parcel of light browns into Japan shows a poor understanding of the market. In the Mideast and Europe, fancy-colored stones and darker stones in the normal ranges do well.

Over the years, there have been many different color classification schemes, or parts of color schemes. In fact, this is an area where, until relatively recently, there was little agreement on what colors really did mean. Over the past few decades, particularly in the United States but even overseas, the so-called GIA color scale has become an industry standard. While this color scale has yet to become the world standard, it has an advantage of having some science behind it. It uses fixed points for color. Most important, it is a framework for explaining other color-naming systems, which developed from tradition rather than science.

The scale starts with idiosyncrasies. The highest diamond rating on this scale is a D (colorless), not an A. It goes down 23 grades to Z, which is a light yellow or brown. Each grade and letter in the scale represents a range of color, not a specific color.

The ranges are close together, and only a practiced eye and a set of carefully graded master stones for comparison will allow you to distinguish a D from an E or an F, particularly in smaller sizes where color does not show up as profoundly. The E and F color grades are so near to colorless that many experienced graders have difficulty on stones under one carat. In stones of a quarter carat (25 points) or less, only the most experienced diamond experts are able to discern the difference. And for the most part, F stones under half a carat are rated *colorless*. In fact, diamonds in the E and F categories are generally called colorless by dealers.

Stones in grades G, H, and I usually exhibit color to trained diamond professionals—but only so long as the stones are unmounted. When mounted, many of these stones appear colorless or *face-up colorless*, even to experienced diamond dealers. This is one of the reasons that knowledgeable dealers in diamonds won't touch a mounted stone and insist that all stones be unmounted before they will evaluate them. Stones in the G, H, I, and J grade are generally classed as *near colorless*.

In grades below I, the color becomes progressively easier to see until, at the bottom end of the scale, virtually anyone can see the depth of color (depending upon the stone size) whether the stone is mounted or not.

In the J, K, and L color grades, all large stones will display traces of color. The flip side of this is that small stones, when mounted, will face up colorless. Diamonds with a color rating of M and below, no matter what the size and whether mounted or not, will display at least a hint of tint to the untrained eye. The GIA grades of K, L, and M are sometimes described as *faint yellow*. Color grades N through R are *very light yellow*, and S through Z are *light yellow*. Stones with color deeper than a Z grade, sometimes called Z+ diamonds, are fancy-colored diamonds.

While this D-Z grading system is employed extensively in the United States, in the foreign fields it is used far less often. Overseas, even though things are changing, you're likely to be offered something like a *Top Silver Cape* or a *Wesselton*. The name really isn't important; the value and the salability of the stone are what count.

No matter what you are offered, you are going to have to grade the color of every stone you are seriously thinking of buying yourself—no matter what system of color grading you use primarily. Nonetheless, it's helpful to know what others are suggesting about the stone's color when they throw out the terms. So if D to Z and beyond seemed pretty straightforward (it will be until you get yourself a set of master stones and actually see how fine-tuned color grading is), let's throw in a couple of other grading systems.

A *Jager* stone in one of the older systems is the name of the top grade. In this system, sometimes called the Jager-to-light yellow or River-to-light yellow, a Jager corresponds to a D-grade diamond. A *River* would be somewhere in the E or F grades; a River is really about two grades wide. The *Top Wesselton* would be a G, and a Wesselton would grade out to an H. A *Top Crystal* is an I, while a *Crystal* corresponds to about a J. The *Top Cape* stone in this system would be comparable to a K or L—this is another classification that is two grades wide. A *Cape* is an M in this system, and a *Low Cape* is about an N color grade. At O and below, diamonds are just *very light yellow* or *very light brown*, with no differentiation.

There is at least one other system that is used widely—one you need to understand because sooner or later someone will start talking to you in these terms. The top grade in this system is *finest white*. For comparison, stones in the top category really cover the D and E color grades. *Fine white* is a term that some would call diamonds in the F and G grades. *White* is equivalent to an H. A *commercial white* stone equals an I-colored diamond. The Top Silver Cape covers everything in the K color and the top half of the K color. The bottom half of the K color and L are interchangeable with a *Silver Cape*. A *Light Cape* would fall into the M and N categories. A *Cape* would grade out anywhere in the O, P, or Q categories and the upper half of the R category. A stone with a color in the bottom half of the R grade or below would be a *Dark Cape*.

At the outset there's not an awful lot of reason to learn all these systems. Choose one, get master stones for it, and use that one. You'll pick up the other systems as you go along; you'll understand the relationships between the different systems when you have to pick them up. For my money, the letter system makes more sense and has more utility as a base system. However, you can use any system as a base and translate it to other color grading systems as need be.

To make things easier for yourself when grading, turn the stones—both master stones and the diamond being graded—onto the stone's table and view them through the bottom, the pavilion. Because of the mechanics of light transmission, the minute color differences are usually more discernible when the stones are viewed through the pavilion or the girdle, the widest part of the stone.

There's a final factor that you have to take into consideration when doing color grading: the environment you'll be working in. That's not to say that you're going to get the ideal environment or anything close to it. The fact is that what you're going to want in terms of light and background is seldom available "in the field" for many transient diamond merchants.

The industry standard for lighting is natural sunlight from a north-facing window. Ha. Far too often you may end up grading by flashlight. There are special lights for diamond grading, available through jewelry supply merchants, that can be carried and used under optimal conditions. Whether this is a wise idea is open to interpretation since the possession of one of these lights is a clear tip-off to Customs authorities and others who are interested that you have a professional or at least serious concern about the minutiae of diamond colors. That leads to embarrassing questions and dangerous conclusions.

In any event, it is important to be aware of the role that light, and even the surrounding environment, have on diamond color, and to try to at least take any probable effect into consideration. It's important to know and remember that brown walls and nearby accoutrements will mask yellows, but blue walls and background surfaces will emphasize the yellow color of diamonds. Always keep the color of the grading environment in mind when buying and grading diamonds; those who don't end up losing.

CLARITY

Clarity is the term that refers to internal or external features called clarity characteristics. Most people simply call them flaws.

Breaks, or visible foreign bodies within a stone, are

inclusions. Imperfections on the outside, such as scratches, are *blemishes.*

Blemishes come in many different sizes and types. The most common types are nicks, knots, scratches, abrasions, minor cracks and cavities, and poor polish. Rarely seen blemishes include a large natural (the unpolished skin of the diamond) and an extra facet, which is visible on or through the crown of the diamond.

The more of these features in or on a stone, the lower the clarity grade and the lower the price. The fact is that while imperfections rapidly lower the clarity grade and send the value plummeting, except in badly flawed stones these clarity characteristics have precious little effect on either the durability or beauty of a stone. Value, remember, is based not on beauty but on rarity.

As with so much in the diamond world, price depends on rarity. The diamond trade caters to the connoisseur. The diamond merchants try to tell the world it has to go along with their definition. It's as if I, for one, like American champagne, which is virtually indistinguishable from the imported product. But the market keeps trying to tell me that I've got to buy the French stuff or I'm not really with it.

The fact is that nothing in nature is ever flawless. So-called flawless stones are flawless only because of a definition: if a trained grader, working with a 10X power magnification under controlled light conditions, can't find a blemish or inclusion, the stone can be called flawless. But that doesn't mean there aren't imperfections in a flawless stone that could be seen with a 20X loupe or 100X magnification. The fact is that there generally are. However, the trade has defined *perfect* to mean that any imperfection has to be visible to a trained grader using 10X magnification.

After perfect there are series of clarity grades. All these grades, down to *imperfect*, contain clarity characteristics that can be seen with a 10X loupe. But with some grades it's hard to find the flaws, and with others it's easy.

At the imperfect grades the flaws and marks are visible with the naked eye, or they affect the durability of the stone. But for every grade between flawless and imperfect, there is really little or no discernible effect on beauty, appearance, or durability. There is just one whopping difference in price.

Below imperfect grades come the *industrial* grades. These are grades so flawed that they are considered, in the trade, only usable for industrial purposes. They are supposed to be priced accordingly. But some unscrupulous jewelers have been buying better-quality industrial-grade rough and having it cut into jewelry-type stones, selling it at what is supposedly a cut rate to people who know no better. Always assume, until you've tested the theory and found it wrong, that any diamond merchant who is selling outside the trade is trying to palm off stones of this quality for an inflated price. And anyone selling to a person he believes might be planning to smuggle the stones is selling outside the trade. Caveat emptor! Remember that just because a stone tests out physically to be a diamond doesn't mean it is a gem-quality stone or that it is valuable.

While the public believes that inclusions are a negative, to those in the diamond trade inclusions are actually a boon in one way. They help separate many of the diamond simulants (fake stones or other types of natural stones used to simulate diamonds) from the real thing. You'll seldom see a purposely produced simulant with any kind of a flaw that appears to be an inclusion. That's about the only positive thing that can be said about inclusions and blemishes, but there is quite a bit more to say about clarity.

A couple of truisms can help guide the beginning grader through the thicket. The size of the fault is probably the most important key to assigning a clarity grade. The easier it is to see an inclusion, particularly when the stone is face up, the greater impact it will have on the clarity grade and the ultimate price.

Linked with the size of inclusions are the number of them and their location. When located in certain parts of the stone, some inclusions will reflect back numerous times in the pavilion. An internal flaw that shows up numerous times as reflections will seriously affect the value of the stone—and its later salability.

Since the clarity grades are better defined than color, it's possible to talk about them with more precision than it is about color.

The apex in the diamond world is *flawless*. This means the stone doesn't have any flaws. Wrong. As explained above, a stone is flawless when no flaws are seen by a skilled grader using a 10X loupe or microscope. *However*—excepted from the no-flaws rule are the following:

- Internal graining that does not affect transparency and is neither whitish, colored, nor reflective.

- Small naturals on the irdle that neither flatten the stone nor affect the symmetry of the diamond.

- Additional facets on the pavilion that are not visible when the stone is viewed face up.

Internally flawless (IF) stones are diamonds without inclusions, but which nonetheless have some minor surface blemishes. In most cases, repolishing the stone would make it flawless.

Extra facets on the crown, large naturals, and surface grain lines are among the features that mark the IF stone.

The next step down is the very very slightly included stones (VVS$_1$ and VVS$_2$). These stones are so slightly flawed that even skilled graders have difficulty detecting the flaws under 10X magnification. Such stones are often sold as flawless by perfectly legitimate sources who just cannot see the minor flaws, which might include slight bearding of the girdle or some internal graining that is reflective. VVS$_1$ inclusions are considered very difficult to see; the inclusions in a VVS$_2$ are only difficult to see!

The flaws in very slightly included stones (VS$_1$ and VS$_2$) are considered to be relatively visible to a trained grader under 10X magnification. While they are slightly difficult to see in a VS$_1$ stone, they are somewhat easy to see in a VS$_2$ stone. Tiny included crystals, small feathers, or pinpoints, are among the various flaws that mark a diamond in this category. For a stone to qualify for a very slightly included rating, none of the flaws must detract from either its beauty or durability.

Slightly included stones (SI$_1$ and SI$_2$) have defects that are fairly easy to see under 10X magnification—but none of the faults may be visible when the stone is viewed face up with the naked eye. Typically the defects in an SI$_1$ are easy to see under 10X magnification, and they are very easy to see in SI$_2$ stones. In some cases in the latter category, the defects are visible to the naked eye when the stone is lying table-down on a piece of white paper. Pits, chips, cavities, feathers, and clouds are among the types of defects often seen in slightly included stones.

Imperfect stones, (I_1, I_2, and I_3) have defects that

- are obvious when viewed under 10X magnification or can be seen with the naked eye,
- affect either brilliance or transparency, or
- could seriously reduce durability, such as large cleavages.

I_3 stones are those in which the entire diamond is heavily included and/or affected by such severe cleavage that the durability is seriously affected.

CUT

Cut is what human beings do to a diamond; each of the other Cs—color, clarity, and carat weight—is essentially a function of nature. Cut makes the diamond beautiful.

Cut is another one of those diamond terms that have a couple of different meanings. When used as one of the Four Cs, it means the *proportions* and *finish* of the diamond rather than facet design or shape.

Proportions are the relationship between the weight distribution, cutting angles, size, shape, and symmetry of a stone. Facet shape, placement, and polish of the stone constitute the finish.

Cutting has evolved over hundreds of years, but it wasn't until the early 20th century that the laws of physics were applied to cutting in order to create a cutting style that balances both *brilliance* and *fire* in a diamond. Unfortunately, relatively few stones are cut to those laws of physics.

When a diamond is cut to the correct proportions, virtually all of the light that enters it will be reflected back out. The light will bounce from facet to facet inside, like a billiard ball caroming off the felt rail. Correct cutting of the diamond to produce these angles of the facets results in brilliance. The fire is caused by refraction, or the bending of the light rays as they pass between mediums of different optical density (i.e., diamond and air). The degree of bending of the light is dependent on the change of the speed, or velocity, of the light as it passes from one medium into another. When the light is bent, the different colors that make up the light are separated into different bands. This shimmering rainbow effect is the fire of a diamond.

But before we go any further, there are a whole lot of terms you need to know and understand.

The three major parts of a modern-cut diamond are the following:

- Crown
- Girdle
- Pavilion

There is a fourth, *culet*, that is often, but not always, found on diamonds.

All modern stones have the three major parts in some form. Like the Four Cs, these names must be as familiar as the words arm or leg. When someone mentions the crown you have to know what he's talking about—without thinking about it. You don't want to ever talk about the "bottom" of a stone when you really mean the pavilion. A single slip of this type betrays you as a neophyte and hence someone to be taken advantage of.

Facets are the plane surfaces of a stone. They are

what give a diamond brilliance and sparkle. Without facets, a diamond is as ordinary looking as a glass marble. (In fact, a marble is much better looking than most uncut and unfaceted diamonds.) The facets of the stone have names. On a Brilliant-Cut diamond the names are table, bezel, star, upper girdle, pavilion main, lower girdle, and culet.

The proportions of a diamond are the ways that the mass of the stone is spread above and below the Girdle. In the most exact use of the term, the proportions include the following:

- Total depth as a percentage of the cirdle diameter
- Table diameter
- Girdle thickness
- Facet angles
- Symmetry
- Finish

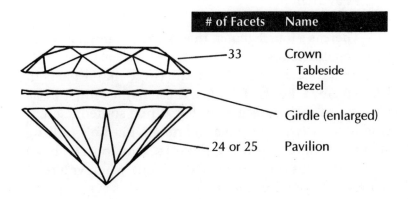

# of Facets	Name
33	Crown
	Tableside
	Bezel
	Girdle (enlarged)
24 or 25	Pavilion

# of Facets	Name
1	Table

8	Bezel facet
	  Crown main
	  Main bezel
	  Kite

8	Star facet

16	Upper girdle facet
	  Break facet
	  Upper or top half

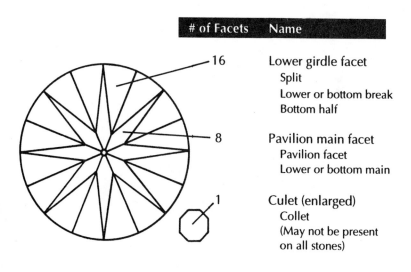

# of Facets	Name

16	Lower girdle facet
	  Split
	  Lower or bottom break
	  Bottom half

8	Pavilion main facet
	  Pavilion facet
	  Lower or bottom main

1	Culet (enlarged)
	  Collet
	  (May not be present
	  on all stones)

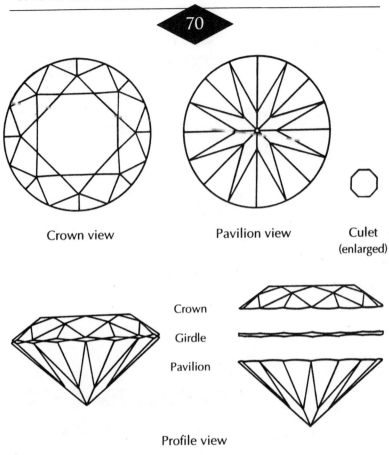

Crown view
Pavilion view
Culet
(enlarged)

Crown

Girdle

Pavilion

Profile view

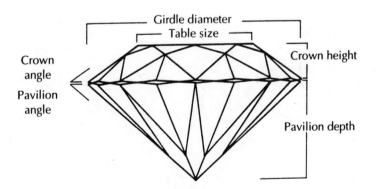

Girdle diameter
Table size
Crown height
Crown angle
Pavilion angle
Pavilion depth

Nearly all diamonds are cut in one of three ways: brilliant, step cut, or mixed. The common thought in the jewelry trade is that the brilliant cut maximizes the brightness of a stone; the step cut shows off the best color; and the mixed cut is a compromise that combines both.

Brilliants are stones in which the facet pattern radiates from the center toward the edge. They have triangular and kite-shaped facets. Brilliants are what we generally think of as "diamonds."

Step cuts have concentric rows of facets that run parallel to the stone's girdle.

Mixed cuts are anything else, a combination of step faceting and brilliant cutting. Often the crown of the stone (the top) and the pavilion (the bottom) are cut in different styles.

Cutting and Hardness

Diamonds' *durability* is high. Durability, in the trade definition, depends upon two factors—*hardness* and *toughness*.

Hardness refers to a stone's ability to be scratched. Toughness is the resistance to cleavage. A diamond is the hardest of all natural stones but has what is known as an octahedral cleavage that is started, or as the diamond cutters say, "developed," fairly easily. Despite that cleavage, it is considered to be among the toughest of gemstones, as well as the pinnacle of hardness.

Natural diamonds are not "grown" in laboratory conditions, with precise measurements of ingredients that produce uniform results. The conditions under which natural diamonds form are dynamic. The temperatures, pressures, and mix of chemicals that produce one lot of diamonds beneath the earth's crust are never quite the same as those that produce another. As a result, the diamond crystals found in nature differ radically from one another. Some crystals become distorted or trapped in the process of crystal growth; impurities among the ingredients can affect both the shape and the color of the diamond.

The diamond cutter gets a piece of rock that can be broken easily at cleavage angles but is hard to saw or cut and often difficult to polish. The cutter's job is to show off the most valuable and sought-after combinations of the diamond rough. The cutter removes, where possible, the less attractive features or tries to conceal them.

The cutter has a hard job working with a hard product—common knowledge is that diamond is the hardest of all materials in nature. Diamonds are indestructible, some believe. Diamonds, so the saying goes, are forever. Diamonds are not forever. They can be seriously damaged or even destroyed. Just dropping a diamond on a desk—if it hits at the wrong angle—can chip it and virtually destroy its value. The public relations genius who coined the phrase about a diamond being "forever" was clearly thinking about what gemologists call scratch hardness. This is a measure of the resistance one stone has to being scratched by another. The Mohs scale is one of the most widely used scratch hardness scales. And in Friedrich Mohs's scale diamonds came out on top. There are different versions of this scale; however, the following is the one most commonly used in the diamond business.

Diamond	10
Corundum	9
Topaz	8
Quartz	7
Feldspar	6

Apatite	5
Fluorite	4
Calcite	3
Gypsum	2
Talc	1

What this all means is that of natural gemstones, only a diamond can scratch another diamond, but it can leave a scratch on all of the other stones with lesser numbers.

The reality is that on a scratch hardness scale, these numbers have no relation to one another. A diamond is nearly 140,000 times harder than talc, while corundum is about 1,000 times more scratch-resistant than talc. But topaz is only about half as scratch-resistant as corundum. The figures in the Mohs scale are not based on any arithmetical or logarithmic progression. It's not a true scale, just an observation as to what stone will scratch what other stone.

Nonetheless, for a long time jewelers and diamond merchants have acted as if the Mohs scale was a good test of the authenticity of a stone they were inspecting. They insisted on using a scratch hardness test to determine whether a particular stone was a diamond. Often they used a stylus-like instrument called a hardness point. Unfortunately, a hardness point stylus, when improperly used, can damage the stone. And many diamonds have been damaged or destroyed because the user didn't understand what he was doing. Other jewel dealers used—and a few still use—the file test. A jeweler's file, which rates about 6.5 on the hardness scale, is supposed to scratch glass but not a diamond. Some jewelers still use this test to detect glass imitations. But the test doesn't prove a stone is a diamond—what it proves is that it is not glass. And since there are a number of harder stones, both natural and artificial, that can be mistaken for diamond, the scratch test fails to deliver a reliable verdict on whether the stone is really a diamond. In addition, even a real diamond can be badly abraded and chipped by the file test if the pressure is applied in a cleavage direction.

The use of a hardness point or a file by any so-called diamond merchant is a clear indication that he's a "never was" who will "never be." Avoid this, unless you want to mark yourself as a rank amateur. That's part of the reason for this long explanation of hardness

There is another reason as well: when you are dealing with diamonds, whether they belong to you or you are carrying them for someone else, remember that diamonds scratch diamonds. When loose stones are kept together they will abrade one another. Seldom is the damage severe, even over a long period, but when you're trying to "deliver the goods," you want to deliver them in the best shape possible.

Under ideal conditions every stone would be in its own *diamond paper*, a specially folded packet. In real life this isn't possible. Particularly when you're moving stones from place to place, a diamond paper is as good as a neon sign to draw attention. (Properly folded diamond papers all too often look like packets of street drugs.) When moving diamonds clandestinely, you will have to discard the papers—trash them in a place where they won't be found and tied to you—and carry the stones in some other way.

It is also impractical to store very small diamonds—the smaller sizes of melee—individually in diamond papers.

There is another quality of stone that gem dealers

call toughness, which is the level of resistance of a stone to chipping, breaking, or cracking. No stone has perfect toughness. And any diamond will fracture, break, and even splinter when hit hard enough and at the right (wrong?) angle. A blow, or even a fall from diamond forceps onto a hard surface, can cause disastrous damage.

Gem dealers rate stones' toughness as poor, fair, good, excellent, and exceptional. Depending upon the angle of the blow, a diamond is generally either rated as good or exceptional in the textbooks. The reality is that when struck in a cleavage direction, a diamond is exceptionally vulnerable: it can and does come apart as easily as sheets of mica.

There is a third term used to describe a diamond's durability, and that is *stability*. Stability is a catch-all category, and it deals with the way the stone stands up to temperature changes, high heat, and chemicals. Overall, diamonds are considered stable. Acid has no effect on them. Cut diamond gems are sometimes affected by heat. Sharp changes in temperature can cause fractures in the stone to extend, though this is relatively rare. Even though diamonds don't burn up like a log in a fireplace (technically, they can be burned under some hard-to-replicate laboratory conditions, but that is not what we're talking about here), high temperatures will mar the surface. "Burned" diamonds can be caused by fires in a home, but they are usually the result of a flub by a jeweler using a torch in his work. This is not a condition that most people involved in moving stones from place to place need to be concerned about. However, if you're buying and selling diamonds you'll eventually run into one of these burned stones, and you need to know what it looks like. When badly burned, they will appear almost opaque. Lesser burns appear to make the stone cloudy. Inexperienced gem handlers will often believe the stone is simply dirty and will try to clean it. When a "dirty" stone looks just as dirty as before after you've cleaned it, think burn. Repolishing is the only way to clean up a burned stone.

Diamonds have an affinity for oil and grease. If there is grease or oil anywhere around, stones will attract it like magnets. In fact, grease tables are one of the methods used to separate diamonds from the surrounding materials in diamond mining. Diamonds will seemingly suck the oil right out of your hands. Soon after they get oily from handling, dirt and dust start adhering to the surface. That really detracts from their beauty, which would be important if you were selling stones to the general public. But oily stones are also more difficult to grade; determining the true value of an oily stone is harder because inclusions tend to appear more prominent. The stone also appears darker, particularly when the diamond is in the lower clarity and color ranges.

For your pocketbook's sake, clean diamonds with lint-free cloths and cleaning solutions before examining them. Ammonia-based cleaning solutions work very well. Some people use alcohol to clean diamonds; it works but it evaporates so quickly that it is hard to use. If you insist on using alcohol, use the right kind. And that means ethyl alcohol. Rubbing alcohol contains enough oil that it dulls the stone and leaves spots.

5

GETTING THE "REAL THING"

IT IS NOT UNKNOWN FOR AN ILLICIT DIAMOND BUYER WHO THINKS HE'S GETTING THE REAL THING to end up paying diamond prices for something like the bottom of a Coke bottle.

Diamond simulants are the bane of every dealer, merchant, and mover of diamonds. Untrained people can discern no difference between diamonds and many of the most common simulants.

The first rule in diamond dealing is to never make assumptions about the identity of a stone—not even if that rock comes with a trunkful of Tiffany pedigree papers. The papers may be accurate, but they may not match the stone.

In the business it is usually, and traditionally, the buyer who makes the first price offer. Be wary if a seller does, particularly if he sets a price at a level that is unbelievably low. Such offers are usually part of a scam—a con game designed to appeal to the diamond buyer's greed. Where the game goes beyond that opening gambit depends. Often the scam is to sell a good-looking diamond simulant, usually mounted in a way that makes it look legitimate, to the buyer at diamond prices. For that reason, a prospective diamond buyer should be concerned about the authenticity of the stone. In a few cases, the would-be seller may be offering a real diamond—but may plan a robbery when cash is produced for the stone.

Experience is a hard teacher. And an expensive one. A few simple lessons will significantly cut the cost of tuition for the school of life.

Remember: diamonds have brilliance, fire, and luster; they are hard. Diamond simulants can imitate some of these qualities, and a few simulants come close to matching many of them. But no simulant can match a diamond in all categories.

When you are checking stones that are represented as diamonds there are any number of tests that can be used, but many test for just one characteristic. A simulant that happens to fall close to the quality you are testing for can convince you, incorrectly, that you've got a gem. For that reason, it's wise to keep a list of the various "diamond indicators" handy and to test for many of them.

- Diamond has a refractive index (RI) of 2.417.

- Its dispersion is .044.

- The luster is called *adamantine*.

- Transparency is exceptional.

- The specific gravity (SG) of diamond is 3.52.

- Hardness, on the Mohs scale, is 10.

- It is tough in cleavage directions and exceptional in all others.

- The fracture pattern is step-line.

- Included crystals are unique.

- Polish can be superior, the best possible.

- Facet edges are usually sharp but on a well-worn stone can be abraded.

- The stone's girdle varies from waxy to granular; bearding is common.

- Naturals on the girdle are growth markings, including triangles and quadrilaterals.

- Spectroscopic exams show absorption at 594, 504, 498, 478, 456, and 415.5 nm.

- Wetability is difficult.

- Thermal inertia is distinctive.

- The response to X-rays is transparent. They almost always fluoresce blue.

These are all diamond indicators. Many of them are useful, but let's face it—you're not going to be hauling spectroscopes around with you. As for luster, someone who is not familiar with adamantine from handling thousands of stones isn't going to find that trait very valuable either. To a very real extent, many of the diamond "markers" are of little use.

But there is help. The diamond tester, or diamond probe as it is sometimes called, is probably the most important piece of equipment a diamond dealer can have. Diamond testers are probably more important than a loupe. These devices test thermal inertia, a quality of diamonds that is distinctive from any of the simulants. The use of a diamond tester is as simple as putting the tip of the probe onto a facet or the table of the diamond. The probe uses a minute amount of electricity and tests the surface temperature for an amount of time when a known amount of heat is added to the stone's surface. There are only a few things that can go wrong—such as the probe tip touching a metal prong of a ring. There are some factors that sometimes need to be taken into account, particularly with some of the more inexpensive models, but none of them require a rocket scientist.

Diamond testers, or probes, range from less than $200 at the lower levels to about $1,000 for the most sophisticated versions. Diamond testers are the first and the most important level of protection that any diamond buyer can use.

It really makes no sense, but all too often the "experts" like to use other tests first and then go to diamond testers for their final decision.

As good as diamond testers are, however, they should never be the sole test used before laying out cash for a stone. Using a loupe, the examiner should be checking for bearding, frosted girdles, and included crystals. When properly identified within a diamond, these are pretty good indicators that the stone is indeed a diamond. Conversely, the appearance of gas bubbles—which can be mistaken for an included crystal—is a pretty good indicator that the stone is a simulant. A knowledgeable grader who understands what a sharp facet and superior polish really are—and far too many people only *think* they know—can often detect simulants because these qualities arise from the hardness of the stone. Diamond simulants, which aren't "as hard as diamonds," just don't "show up" sharp facet edges and polish in the same way.

After that, a check of specific gravity is often used. Since most of the common diamond simulants have higher specific gravity than diamonds, this is a good test. However it will not work on some glass simulants and on some doublets.

Checking for high dispersion is a good test of a diamond; however, cubic zirconia, synthetic rutile, and strontium titanate have significantly more dispersive qualities and can, on that basis, be mistaken for diamonds.

Refraction is a useful, but often confusing, test for diamonds. Diamond is singly refractive. Some simulants, such as synthetic sapphire, synthetic rutile, and zircon, are doubly refractive. On the other hand, simulants with refractive indexes below that of strontium titanate show a read-through (nonrefractive) effect.

Simulants have been around virtually since someone discovered that diamonds were valuable. Some of the desire for simulants was quite benign. People who couldn't afford the "real thing" wanted to pretend that they could, and they bought things that could be passed off as diamonds. Some of the use of simulants came about as a result of greed. If you sell a stone that costs you very little and get a high price, you've made lots of money. Crooks learned early on that there was money to made by bamboozling the buyer.

What is probably the oldest diamond simulant is zircon, a natural gemstone that comes in a variety of colors—and some of it is colorless.

The earliest mass-manufactured simulants were glass with a heavy dose of lead oxide. Often these were foil-backed—a thin strip of metallic foil was added to the backs of these diamonds to reflect more light out the front of the stone. *Paste,* the word used to describe many of these early diamond simulants, is still used in the diamond trade today when referring to glass simulants. Rhinestones are simulants made from quartz rocks; the name came from the fact that the quartz for these was first mined in the Rhine Valley. Modern rhinestones are foil-backed as well, but not by using the old methods. Instead of foil some type of mirroring film—it is often seen as a sort of golden or dark-colored paint on the back of rhinestones—is applied. This is used by some of the more successful diamond smugglers in their movement of stones, something we will go into at length later in the book.

Glass doublets were probably the next major improvement in the fakery department. At first a garnet top was fused to a glass bottom. The thin top took the color (or the lack of color) of the glass base and made a creditable stone. Doublet-making has become far more sophisticated these days. Doublets are increasingly hard to detect as advances in fakery are barely matched by improvements in detection equipment.

There is a new use for glass that the diamond buyer—particularly one who isn't going to be able to bring back the gems himself—has to be aware of. Liquid glass is sometimes used on diamonds to cover up noticeable cracks, a relatively new process known as fracture filling. Done professionally, it may take a close look to detect, but keep in mind that the difference between such a doctored stone and a diamond without a crack is a major one. So that close look can be important. Unfortunately, there are more than a few people who would like to pocket the difference in value between what is essentially a nice-colored, well-cut industrial-grade diamond and a high-quality stone. You may well meet people who like to get that difference in value out of your pocket. Caveat emptor!

Besides the obvious, there are a variety of other common substitutes. All of them have a legitimate place in the glittering world of jewelry. But each can also be used to bamboozle a buyer—even sophisticated buyers.

ZIRCON

Natural zircon that has no color is fairly rare. While the substitution of zircon for diamonds is an old trick, as old as the hills, it had never been widespread until the 20th century. Colorless zircon was just too rare for that to happen. However, early in the 1900s someone found that heat treatments were effective in removing the color from zircon. At that point zircon became the simulant of choice, and the best at the time.

Zircon has a major advantage over glass. It has much more brilliance. It also has enough fire that it can often be slipped in as a diamond simulant. A key point for the wary buyer to remember is that one result of the heat treatment of zircon—to make it colorless—is that it also becomes very brittle. Because of the heat treatment a set stone abrades easily. Zircon simulants can often be detected by a close examination of the facet junctions, which tend to get scratched and rounded off.

SYNTHETIC RUTILE

Rutile is a natural stone, but in nature it is extremely rare to find transparent, nearly colorless, gem-quality stones. However, a synthetic form of this stone, produced commercially, took over as the diamond simulant in the 1940s and 1950s.

Although it lacks the brilliance of diamonds, this crystalline form of titanium oxide is brilliant enough that people who don't deal with diamonds on a daily basis may mistake it for a diamond. A giveaway for synthetic rutile is that it is highly dispersive—its rainbow-like quality is so strong that even people who are not diamond experts sometimes question it because it seems far too dispersive. It is low on the hardness scale, and that means that anything but a new stone will show signs of wear that would not be found on a diamond. Synthetic rutile tends to have a yellowish cast, which may or may not be a clue. Many diamonds are slightly yellowish as well.

If you want to get a piece of synthetic rutile to test for yourself (it's always a good idea to have experience with simulants), the stone is known by a number of trade names, including Diamothyst, Kenyagem (Kima gem), Kimberlite gem, Rainbow gem or diamond, Star-Tania, Titan gem, Titanium, and a variety of names having derivatives of Titanium in the name.

STRONTIUM TITANATE

The natural counterpart for this stone was not identified until nearly 30 years after the chemical compound first hit the market. It, like diamond, is singly refractive. It is nearly colorless, which makes it much more useful as a diamond simulant, and it has dispersive qualities that, although they exceed that of diamonds, are more in the order of diamonds than synthetic rutile. For those reasons it quickly became a substitute of choice. Strontium titanate lacks durability, hence older stones will show wear relatively quickly. Even though other simulants have now outclassed it, strontium titanate still shows up in the gem market, often as a doublet with a synthetic sapphire table.

To get a piece look for trade names such as Diagem, Dynagem, Fabultine, Lustigem, Marvelite, Wellington, and Zenithite.

YAG

YAG, or yttrium aluminum garnet, revolutionized two industries: lasers and diamond simulants.

This artificial crystal—it has no counterpart in nature—is made to resemble the crystalline structure of garnet. It has a relatively good, but not adamantine, brilliance factor and a hardness that, while not that of diamond, is impressive (8.25 on Mohs scale).

A major drawback is that it lacks the same fire, the dispersive qualities, of diamond.

It is often sold simply as YAG, but it is also known by a number of trade names, including Amatite, Alexite, Diamogem, Diamonair, Diamonique, Di-yag, Linde, and Triamond.

GGG

Sometimes used as a diamond simulant is a man-made garnet called gadolinium gallium garnet, mercifully shortened by everyone in the business to GGG. Its major fault is that it is relatively soft and scratches easily. But it is more brilliant and more dispersive than YAG.

SYNTHETIC CUBIC ZIRCONIA

Of all the simulants to date, this is the best. It has

the brilliance or luster of diamond but a little more fire, though few people, including professionals, would note that, With a hardness of up to 8.5, it has relatively good durability. In short, it looks like a diamond and acts like a diamond in many respects.

Synthetic Cubic Zirconia is known widely as CZ; other trade names include Diamonique II and Phyanlite.

SYNTHETIC DIAMONDS

Synthetic diamonds are diamonds. They are made in a laboratory. Gem grade synthetics have not proven economically competitive with natural diamonds but may well become so in the near future. However, remember that diamond simulants are not synthetic diamonds, nor are synthetic diamonds simulants.

TRICKS OF THE TRADE

Buying simulants isn't the only way to be cheated. Any time you have your own stones out, whether they are master stones or you are selling, you're vulnerable.

Making certain that you don't get ripped off by unscrupulous people who want to examine your stones is important—and easier to do than you think.

When dealing with *anyone* and showing diamonds, put the stone in a locking tweezers—one that is distinctively marked—or a stone holder rather than in diamond papers.

The basic rule is to stay alert and not let people distract you from the stone. Whether you're selling or buying, the stone itself has to be your focus. Those trying to sell you a simulant will try to distract you so that you accept only the surface indications that it is a diamond.

Those trying to rip you off when you are selling may be trying to replace your genuine diamond with a simulant.

You can never assume any stone to be a diamond—even one you've had in your stock and shown over and over again. Any time a stone is removed from a case and passed to a potential buyer, it has to be assumed that it is a fake until you can verify that it is the same stone.

CHAPTER

THE TRIP

FOR SOMEONE WHO IS JUST STARTING INTO THE BUSINESS OF BUYING, MOVING, AND SELLING DIAMONDS, there are two big questions:

- Who do I buy from?
- Who do I sell to?

No one can answer those questions with any specificity. Diamond merchants change their habits as time goes on, as they acquire new contacts, face new challenges, and meet new people. Diamond merchants do not stay with the same people throughout their careers. The rule is to patronize a source as long as it can give you the best deal; the corollary rule is to make sure you always get as good a deal as you can because you've got to give your clients the best deal possible if you're going to keep them.

If you're a buyer, you may be doing business in some fly-infested swamp, talking pidgin French to a native digger who is offering what he says is a diamond. Or you may be working the diamond bourses and clubs of a cutting center such as Antwerp or Tel Aviv.

Where you have a choice, if you have the choice, take the bourses. The people you'll deal with there are every bit as cutthroat on the boulevards as they are in bush, but you probably won't have to compete with DeBeers when you're working the cutting centers.

In the world of diamonds, a field that has more of the trappings of a religion than of a business, the bourse is the college of cardinals. It is here that the hierarchy of the diamond world congregates, carrying parcels of diamonds worth literally millions of dollars.

There is almost a score of major bourses. Some cities have more than one. Antwerp, for instance, has four. Major bourses are located in London, New York, Antwerp, Tel Aviv, Milan, Paris, Singapore, and Vienna, as well as other major cities.

Some of the bourses specialize in polished stones, others deal in rough. The bourse, or diamond club as some call it, is more than an exchange, though many people would liken one to a stock or mercantile exchange.

In fact, the bourse is a country all of its own, with rules and regulations that are practically inviolate. It has its own code of conduct, and it deals with the people within its walls as a medieval parish would have done. Its people may be stern and harsh toward local transgressors, but the members will stonewall outsiders when it comes to matters that relate to other members. When disagreements occur between members, the leaders of the bourse handle the situation in their own ways. There is no need to turf the matter to some law court—the members of the bourse arbitrate the matter for the parties.

If the matter reaches beyond a simple disagreement, if it is more in line with something that a criminal court should handle, that too is taken care of by the bourse. It can suspend or even expel errant members. Since all of the bourses worth going to belong to a world federation of bourses, and since all the bourses will honor suspensions and expulsions without exception, the home bourse has tremendous powers. Suspension or expulsion by a bourse may not be able to put a diamond trader completely out of the business, but one can reduce a champagne life-style to a beer budget.

The bourse's laws, most of them unstated, do not follow the civil law. Rather there is a single rule—always behave with integrity toward other members of the bourse. Once a deal is done, the behavior of the buyer or seller outside the walls of the diamond club is irrelevant. However, inside the walls, a man's word is stronger than any piece of paper; a hand clasp means more than a signature.

One key thing to remember about trading on the bourse is that you are dealing with an individual, with a single person. Companies aren't represented on the bourse. The men who congregate at a bourse are individuals. Frankly, most Americans will find that they have a different social and sexual ethic. Not better. Not worse. Just different. For the diamond bourse is a man's club. Women just are not accepted in this trade.

The bourse is a closed club with admission requirements every bit as stringent, though not as bloodthirsty, as La Cosa Nostra. In general, bourse applicants must have at least two years of trading experience behind them. They have to be sponsored by one or more people who are already members of the bourse. After an applicant's interrogation by a board that functions as a membership committee, his application is thrown out for all members of the bourse to challenge. Even if unchallenged, the membership is far from permanent. Even when admitted, new members remain on a sort of probation for their first two years of membership.

If there is a lingua franca of the bourse, it is Yiddish. Even members of the diamond fraternity who follow faiths other than Judaism know basic Yiddish. When diamond deals are made, they are traditionally sealed with a handshake and the Yiddish phrase for "luck and blessings," *mazel u'bracha*.

Diamond sellers—diamantaires as they are called in the trade—do most of their business at the long tables that nuzzle up to the windows in a bourse's main room. By tradition, the high windows face north so that they afford the best, most consistent natural light for examining the stones.

Though they are steeped in tradition and are throwbacks socially, bourses have not ignored the modern world. Most have modern communications equipment of all kinds, a communications suite that would make a small military force envious. And while their main rooms are the key to trades, they have smaller offices where they can lock up the deal. Those offices afford the dealers some degree of privacy for negotiations. Bourses also have state-of-the-art security that is seldom breached from outside.

A typical bourse may have 1,000 or 2,000 members—though not all of the people will be in the main room on any given day. It is the bourse members who function as the first truly free market in the diamond chain. Before them is DeBeers, and after them is a web of sellers and resellers that finally ensnares a love-struck couple who believe, or at least hope, that a diamond is forever.

The chances are against your becoming a member of a bourse. That said, you'll need to contact wholesalers. Wholesalers may be a company or a single individual. Some will buy from many cutters and sell to anyone who comes along. Others may buy from a single cutter and limit their sales to other dealers.

Having friends who can tell you who the dealers are and their specialties is important. Even better than information are introductions. For people who are moving diamonds from one location to another, their source may be a wholesaler in Belgium, Brazil, Israel, or India, and their client may be (will probably be) a wholesaler in their home country.

For most dealers who specialize in moving stones internationally, it's a matter of knowing *who* as much as *what*—and the who has to be learned by some process other than a book. The diamond trade is based on trust, and no text can be a substitute for the personal trust. Letters, or letters and phone calls, of introduction are the key that opens doors, and diamond papers, to you.

As for payment, until they know you *very* well, virtually all wholesalers want to see your money before they hand you a parcel of diamonds. Don't expect to get the stones on credit, or, in the diamond argot, "on memo." That means you need to work out, in advance, how you are going to transfer the money to pay for the diamonds.

Cash talks. Enough said.

Getting a good deal depends on many different factors. Having cash at the ready is one. But there are others.

Since grading is a time-consuming business and time is money, many buyers who are good at grading improve their buying power by patronizing dealers who keep their costs lower by selling stones they haven't carefully sorted themselves. For graders who know what they're doing, this is a worthwhile tactic. For neophytes at the business, buying into ungraded parcels can be a ticket to disaster.

A buyer who can take a large parcel off a wholesaler's hands and give him money in return will generally fare better financially than one who buys a small selection of stones. With a bulk buyer the wholesaler doesn't have to take the time to sell the rest of his goods to other customers. It saves him time and energy.

In this business, time equates to money and the wholesaler can give part of that back to you—if you bargain with him for it.

Whereas your activities overseas and the places you go are important, the fact is that it's the small things you do before you ever leave home that can make or break your business.

The military refers to it as preparation for overseas movement, or POM. When going on a business trip, the diamond mover and merchant has to plan as meticulously and prepare as thoroughly as any military force. A failure to do so has the same consequences it would to a military force—capture or worse.

The first consideration is how many of you there will be on the trip. Single-person efforts are more common, more profitable, and less involved. They are also much more risky.

Having a two-person team is the best way. That doesn't mean that the two people should travel together or stay together. In fact, the two should go separately, starting from different cities and on different flights when possible. They stay at different hotels or lodgings, generally fairly near to one another, in the same city.

The one-man show can cause serious problems for

the diamond merchant who is not playing strictly by the book. This is because the gear you need to carry with you—loupes, scales, diamond testers, among others—are a clear signal to any customs agents or baggage inspectors that you're interested in expensive stones. Even the dullest public servant at home or abroad can put two and two together—and if it's noted that you're carrying loads of jewelry equipment on entering a country, that information may get passed along to the powers that be. Just a note in a file, or adding your name to a typed list of people who deserve extra attention upon leaving or entering, can be dangerous. In such a case, ditching the equipment when leaving—an expensive proposition—won't even be of much help. Customs agents may well have already noted to give you special attention on leaving. The lack of equipment and supplies in that case under those circumstances will only highlight the clandestine nature of your activities and make authorities more curious.

But that's getting ahead of the game. The diamond mover should have a vouched-for contact before leaving home. Trying to go overseas and "find" someone to deal with is the surest road to disaster imaginable.

The diamond mover needs to find out as much about the city where the transaction will take place as he can. If he's never traveled to that particular location, a thorough and serious study of maps and travel books (available at large bookstores or through map makers' catalogues), as well as careful coordination with travel agents, are required. Discussions with people who have been there before can be most helpful.

Although written words never replace actual experience, the diamond merchant can get a fair idea of the overall danger level in the area he is going to by consulting the State Department's Consular Affairs hotline and fax service for information.

These reports generally contain information on entry requirements, locations of embassies and consulates in the United States, crime information, security data, and usually the phone number and address of the U.S. consulates in the area where you'll be working. That information, particularly the consulate information, is invaluable if a problem arises.

That information is available by calling the State Department Bureau of Consular Affairs automated fax system at (202) 647-3000 from a Touch Tone phone. You'll get further instructions on the line. If they're confusing, get the list of publications. You order that sent to your fax by pressing the star (*) key, then the number (#) key, and when you are told, the start or connect button. Once you've received the list—it's about six to ten pages in length—review it for the information you need. Then order the information you need.

There is another State Department fax number that can provide useful "background notes" on selected countries: (202) 736-7720.

Use this service, but use it wisely and be discreet about it.

It is important to prepare for the worst—getting busted overseas. The Consular Affairs hotline is apparently no stranger to people who have legal problems, and they have a set of reports on the court system for many countries overseas. It is always wise to check whether your country is covered.

When you use a team of two persons, the one who will make all the contacts carries the equipment in and out. That person does the bargaining and buying, evaluates the stones, and passes the money. When the bargainer gets possession of the diamonds, he then passes the goods over to the second person—the courier—who will actually move the diamonds out of the country and into another nation.

The courier serves in a number of other capacities. The courier is not a mule who lugs the load but has to be a calm professional. Most important, the courier is a backup to the buyer if the buyer gets in trouble, for instance, or disappears. In the event of trouble, the courier notifies friends or relatives back in the United States and has them formally start a search, contact diplomatic officials, get a lawyer, and so on.

The courier in a team, at all times, maintains a strict separation from the purchaser. Messages are passed between the buyer and courier through blind drops and innocuous codes whenever necessary. The two can see one another, and probably should see one another, at least once a day. But except for the necessary communication of information through drops and codes, and the one-time passing of the stones, the two should never even acknowledge the presence of one another.

The once-a-day security and safety check should be planned in advance so that both of the parties will be lunching in the same cafe, walking down the same street, at the same time, on the correct day. This is a visual check on health and welfare only, and the two people never make verbal or other contact at this time.

The purchaser makes the contacts, examines the stones, and makes the financial arrangements for the transfer of the stones to him. After the stones are in the hands of the buyer, he drops contact with the seller and transfers the diamond or diamonds, usually at some brief meeting. For instance, the two might arrange to sit on a bus next to one another. The package of stones can be transferred through a rolled-up newspaper that the buyer gives the courier, who asks if he can read the newspaper. There are numerous similar methods of handing off the stones; this is only given as an example.

The hand-off is the only time the two should ever talk to one another, except in an emergency.

The buyer, having disposed of his goods to the courier, can then go about doing other things. Perhaps the buyer will travel elsewhere or catch a plane to depart for home.

When using a two-person team approach, the buyer should always leave the country first and return to the country where the stones are being brought in first.

Why? The buyer is clean; the buyer is carrying no stones. But at least one person, the seller, knows who the buyer is, and the authorities may know as well. The fact is that far too many sellers play a two-faced game. They will sell stones to a buyer whom they suspect will not be declaring the stones properly and then quietly inform the authorities about the transaction. The authorities search the buyer's belongings, and person if need be, and, "fortuitously," just happen to turn up the stones. The seller has his money. The authorities have their man. And everybody's happy except the unlucky buyer who no longer has the stones or the money—but is facing a hefty legal bill.

When the buyer goes home first, if the courier and the buyer have been circumspect in their contacts, the authorities will probably have no inkling of where the stone or parcel actually is. They will most likely assume that the buyer has possession of it and will search him thoroughly. Extra special attention to the buyer by Customs authorities when he returns to his home country is a tip-off that someone, probably the diamond seller, has been talking. It is also a signal that the courier should be taking extra special precautions since someone knows that there are some diamonds on the loose.

To confuse Customs authorities, some buyers seek out the places where international air crews stay and recreate, then make a special point of making friends as "one American to another," or something along those lines. Since much of the International Diamond Smuggling (IDS) done these days involves members of flight crews, the contact between the diamond buyer and any member of a flight crew sets tailing Customs officials off on a wild goose chase, thinking that they see through the ploy.

What should the buyer and the courier be doing overseas, and what reason do they have for being where they are? Good cover stories are essential. The unvarnished truth will never do! Even if everything is done in accordance with the laws and customs of every country conceivably involved in the transaction, it is foolish to advertise that you are on a diamond-buying (or selling) trip. Crooks can smell money, and if they smell the kind of money that it takes to buy diamonds, even on a black or gray market, you're in danger from another direction. That's a direction where scruples don't count.

The mention of the word scruples brings us down to another issue—snitches.

There is often a very real reason for someone to turn a diamond smuggler in—the money they can get. The power of this incentive is clear from a 1994 incident in Sierra Leone where the government offered 40 percent of a subsequent sale price as a "fee." In due course, along came some illegal Lebanese dealers who acquired a 172-carat stone. Not long afterward, acting on a tip, police seized the diamond and the dealers. A month later the stone sold for $2.83 million. You can live right nicely on 40 percent of $2.83 million I'm told.

Snitchery is a way of life in DeBeers country. And DeBeers country is anywhere it says it's interested in. Some people feel perfectly confident in going into DeBeers territory and trying to beard the diamond devil in his den. You won't be getting that kind of advice here.

DeBeers controls *most* of the diamond business, from mining to what are, in effect, wholesale sales at the cartel's sights. It doesn't control *all* of that business and may not want to have a lock on it *all*, though the latter comment is just kindly speculation. The fact is that most people in the field feel that DeBeers gets a little testy about people coming in and buying from illegal miners; the company seems to become a bit upset about stones that go outside its channels anywhere along the line during the first part of the diamond chain.

It is not surprising that most people in the business feel that DeBeers's agents hear about anything and anybody dealing in diamonds. And if DeBeers's people hear about free-lancers in the field, and if they got up on the wrong side of the bed that morning, and if their superiors are telling them that a few too many stones are getting away, then . . .

In fairness, DeBeers agents probably aren't as dangerous as the trade talk tends to paint them. But why take chances with the rest of your life? DeBeers has been accused of just about everything imaginable, including promoting a civil war in Angola so that wildcat diggers and stone poachers could exploit the alluvial deposits while DeBeers buyers soaked up the liberated stones like a sponge absorbs water.

Supporters of the DeBeers monopoly—and there are many, especially high up in the government of almost every country where DeBeers does business—seem to have a different view of the company that is more a country than a cartel. Their view is benign. Such supporters of DeBeers would maintain that the monopoly just had to gather in those stones from wildcat diggers in Angola. Why, they'll tell you, the monopoly's firm action stabilized prices for investors and engagement ring buyers alike while it kept up the quality of diamonds being sent for cutting. Noblesse oblige! What a great bunch of guys.

Whatever others say, just remember: DeBeers's people act on behalf of no government. They are not responsible to any voters. They have to follow no constitution. They have no constraints except success, success at keeping all the stones inside their own economic pipeline. They may tell you they have to follow the law of whatever country they're in. Even if that's true, there's no reason, if you get in their way, that they should not cheerfully turn you in to Customs or whatever agency they have reason to believe may have jurisdiction over you and your future.

The bottom line—the one that's good for your bottom as well as your bottom line—is don't mess with DeBeers until you've got as many employees, as much money, and as many governments under contract as it has. It is smartest to confine your transactions to the area DeBeers seems less concerned about. Forget about dealing in diamond rough; deal with finished stones and you'll find that your path isn't strewn with the most explosive of land mines.

CHAPTER

MOVING THE GOODS

THE LIST OF WAYS TO MOVE STONES WITHOUT DETECTION IS INEXHAUSTIBLE. The methodologies of smuggling are so vast that the largest diamond firms don't even try to second-guess the would-be smugglers.

At diamond mine sites, particularly in areas where diamonds can be most easily found by workers without anyone else being aware, it's as though the mine operators simply defy some law of gravity. What goes up must come down, but what goes into one of those sites does not come out. The diamond mine area is like a black hole, pulling in items that will never be seen again.

Vehicles, consumer goods, even some children's toys, may be imported into the mine zone. However, they do not leave again. Workers, when they leave, may be able to take their clothes and a few valued items—but only after lengthy inspections (of days, not hours). Vehicles have too many nooks and crannies in which to hide diamonds. Any vehicles that have ever been inside the mine area remain there. Period. Vehicles from outside are not allowed to enter the area; visiting drivers leave their own vehicles outside and get a vehicle owned by the diamond mine at the gate. They can drive that inside the mine compound but must leave it inside the gate and pick up their own cars when they go out again.

Large consumer goods are just as hard to search effectively as a car, and for that reason they too remain inside the fence once they are brought in.

Children's toys seem to be a favorite with smugglers who hope to rely on the warm and fuzzy feelings adults have toward kids in order to conceal contraband. For that reason, Customs agents and others involved in anti-smuggling operations worldwide will zero in on toys, particularly stuffed toys, whenever they see them. Some in the business—perhaps the brassiest in the business—will carry a stuffed teddy bear in their luggage. If a Customs agent has any inkling that the person may be carrying undeclared merchandise, that teddy bear is like a lightning rod. They'll go right to it and will sometimes become terribly frustrated when they don't find anything. After tearing the stuffed bear apart, squeezing out your toothpaste, and so on, they'll be muttering under their breath when they let you go.

This is one of the reasons why a two-person team makes the most sense when moving stones from one country or location to another. If the authorities have been tipped off, they'll search the person who was identified as the buyer from attic to cellar. They *know* the guy bought something, but they can't risk disclosing the source of their information. They have to make it appear that, just by dumb luck and good intuition, they stumbled across the smuggled goods. (When, as the authorities occasionally do with a big haul, they put out a statement or press release crediting luck, you can usually bet money they're trying to cover a snitch.)

When the buyer of a team undergoes an exceptionally thorough search by Customs on arrival back in his country, that's a pretty solid clue that they were just waiting—waiting because someone told them something. That's the time when a decision has to be made whether to keep the stones offshore for a little while, waiting for things to cool down in the ice business, or whether to rely on the courier's wits, imagination, talent, and intelligence to bring the shipment in anyway.

Who makes the best courier? It has to be someone who blends in, who can give a good reason to be outside the country. Members of ship or air crews are among the most sought-after couriers in the business. Their work-a-day jobs are a natural camouflage for their operations.

The sex of the courier isn't as important as other factors; both men and women can be flighty, nervous types, which is the last thing you want in a diamond courier. Customs officials don't seem to favor either men or women in their searching. Of course, if you're planning on a body cavity carry, then obviously women are twice as qualified as men, particularly at certain times of the month when Customs agents may not be as careful as they should be about inspecting everything.

From my experience women, as a whole, often perform better under stress than men. They have a better intuitive sense of problems and possible solutions. Women, for a number of reasons having to do with their perceived role in life and society's norms, have had a great deal more experience in saying the right thing, in choosing the right tone, than men. They know better than men when to be aggressive and can play a passive role far more effectively than any man. For my money, women couriers are far better than men.

If your courier doesn't have a great alibi job—air or ship crew member, for instance—then it is important to develop, learn, and live a good cover. Women are really very good at going abroad innocuously, claiming they're looking up genealogical records, and actually making that story stick. (That, by the way, is one of the better ones to explain what you're doing on your travels—provided you've thoughtfully included *correct* genealogical research materials in your luggage.)

But no matter what the cover, no matter who the courier, there comes that moment of truth when someone has to go through Customs.

Unless you're doing an invoicing scam and declaring the diamonds (but declaring them as less valuable grades and colors), you can't admit that you have the stones when you enter the country. They either have to be (1) invisible (sealed in a toothpaste tube or carried in a tampon, for instance) or (2) camouflaged so that they will be mistaken for something else. Most smugglers of stones opt to make them invisible. My belief has always been that it is best to put things out in plain view.

For the people who prefer to make them invisible, Appendix B is a list, obtained in a roundabout manner, from a U.S. government agency of likely places where contraband may be hidden. Frankly, it would seem to be folly to use anything on that list—these are the places the inspectors are trained to look. Nonetheless, I know people who do all right with the hidey-holes found in the appendix.

If you believe, as I do, that the smartest move is to put the stones out for all to see, you'll develop some much different techniques.

In some cases, just before going overseas it's easy to make a declaration to Customs that you intend to take your foreign-made camera, your Rolex watch, and several valuable pieces of personal jewelry (rings, pins, or other jewelry if appropriate people are going with you). The items are as described—the stones in the rings are diamonds of good color, cut, and quality, and about the size you intend to bring back. After registering the items it's not hard to quickly unmount the actual stones, pass them to a friend seeing you off, and slap in pieces of good paste in their place.

Once you have acquired several parcels of the good-quality stones overseas you can unmount all the fakes, replace them with the real stones, and travel back—declaring part of the diamond purchases, the part that is still in diamond papers. It's important to make certain that all the paperwork matches the stones you are declaring, and that the camera, watch, and jewelry declared on the way out match the items brought back in. You pay for the declared stones and show the outgoing declaration, and everyone seems happy. But you'll be happiest of all.

This method requires a little skill in stone setting, as well as some basic jewelry-setting tools and findings. When a courier's help is available, you can use a variation on the theme that actually requires little jewelry knowledge.

Carry over some medium-range costume jewelry—good enough that it clearly isn't five-and-dime quality, but not so good that even the densest of Customs agents can't tell that it is fake. Again, after you have purchased the new stones overseas, the fake stones are removed from the pieces of costume jewelry and the real diamonds are set—quite often literally glued—in their place. Often, the smartest smugglers will carefully paint the pavilion of the diamonds with gold paint. This changes their optical properties, making them seem less than adamantine, and conforms to the way that some paste stones are backed. A note of caution needs to be sounded here, however: if you paint or treat the backs of any of the stones in a piece of costume jewelry, do it to them all. Make certain that the backs of all the stones match.

The piece (sometimes pieces) of costume jewelry is then passed to the courier at the one "meet" allowed per trip. The courier brings the diamond-bearing costume jewelry back with a jumble of other costume pieces. (A woman can bring it back as her own; a male courier needs to say that it is gift for a wife or girlfriend and should have a sales slip for a piece of costume jewelry that generally matches what would be the expected value of the jewelry.) This method works well when dealing in batches of stones of smaller-size (.5 or .75 carat) or multicarat stones. Larger diamonds can be foil-backed with red, green, or blue foil to give them the illusion of being fake rubies, emeralds, or sapphires, or their color can be changed with paint on the backs.

In any event, the stones are hidden in plain sight. They are in the last place most Customs agents expect them to be—in front of their noses.

Other variations of this tactic are to sew or glue the diamonds—made to look like fake stones by coating the backs—to other forms of clothing. Souvenir hats or caps "feminized" for women by the addition of rows of "rhinestone" diamonds are one way of bringing stones back. Real diamonds can be substituted for rhinestone decorations on virtually any piece of clothing, or any other item for that matter. Men can get away with bringing back gaudy jewelry boxes, ornaments, and so on, as "gifts." But again, it's always important to declare the items and have some kind of invoice or receipt to verify that you did, indeed, buy the item abroad.

The key to all these methods is simple—no one expects you to be smuggling anything as part of something you took out of the country, or as part of something that you have declared.

THE LAST WORD

WHATEVER YOU DO IN THE FUTURE, REMEMBER TO LEAVE THIS BOOK AT HOME WHEN YOU GO OVERSEAS. There are few things that are more likely to get your bags ripped apart, stitch by stitch, at Customs than the discovery of this book in your luggage.

You might also have to submit to numerous physical indignities, such as body searches, when they don't find anything. In any event, you're likely to be late for your connecting flight!

And remember—under no circumstances admit to anyone that you have ever smuggled so much as a matchstick. Honesty is never the best policy when it comes to Customs officers.

And—*mazel tov*!

GLOSSARY

Adamantine—A term describing the luster of a diamond, and only a diamond.

Alluvial stones—Rough stones of any kind, including diamonds, that have been carried by water and deposited on shores, in the sea, in lakes, or along stream beds. Alluvial stones may be found in dry areas that were once under water or were formerly the course of rivers and streams. The largest alluvial diamond recorded was found in Sierra Leone in 1972, the Star of Sierra Leone, weighing some 970 carats.

American cut—See ideal cut.

Baguette cut—A type of step cutting. Small rectangular or trapeze-shaped gems, including diamonds, are cut in the baguette style.

Base—The same as a pavilion of a stone, the portion of the diamond below the girdle.

Bearded girdle—A girdle that lacks the waxy luster and smoothness of a well-fashioned stone, often because it was *rounded up* without care. This type of girdle, which will sometimes be termed rough, has a granular appearance. Often the fashioning process has created many tiny hairline fractures extending into the stone from the girdle, hence being bearded. This is sometimes called a *fuzzy girdle*.

Bezel—The sloping top surface of the diamond down to, but not including, the girdle. Often, it is used correctly to describe the entire portion of a brilliant-cut gemstone above the girdle. When the word is used in this manner it is synonymous with crown.

Bezel facets—On a brilliant-cut gem, the eight crown facets that touch the table with the top points and the girdle with the bottom points.

Black center—In some diamonds, ones with an extra thick pavilion, the angles allow light that should be reflected back out the top to leak through the bottom. This causes the stone to have a dark center. This black center, referred to by some dealers as a *well*, is caused by a cutter attempting to retain extra weight by refusing to cut to ideal proportions.

Blemish—An imperfection on the surface of a diamond.

Bourse—Diamond sales club, usually restricted to males, in major diamond markets.

Break facets—In a round, brilliant-cut stone, these are the 32 facets that touch the girdle, half of them above and the other half below the girdle. Also called girdle facets.

Brilliant cut—The cutting of a diamond most popularly associated with the gem. The brilliant cut has 32 facets and a table on the crown, the area above the girdle. It has 24 facets and a culet below the girdle, on the pavilion.

Bruise—A term diamond dealers use for a mark on a stone that results from a sharp impact. It is often seen as a small whitish mark on the stone, sometimes with a four- or six-sided shape. *Percussion mark* is another term for this.

Carbon—Any inclusion in a diamond that appears black, particularly if it can be seen without magnification. They key word here is *appears* black. The term does not mean that the inclusion is either carbon or is actually black.

Carbonado—A type of diamond that gem dealers do not have to deal with. However, for diamond merchants who deal in industrial-grade materials, this is the apex. Carbonado is a mass of minute diamond crystals—often black, brown, or grayish in color—and is considered to be the toughest form of diamond. It is highly sought after for many industrial purposes.

Comparison stones—These are fashioned stones of known color grades used to compare with stones being graded to determine body color. Sometimes called master stones or, less frequently, key stones, these are essential in color grading. Despite the claims of some that they can remember colors, the vast majority of the evidence shows that relying on memory to grade the subtle colorations of diamonds will eventually turn out to be a costly mistake.

Crown—The top surface of a diamond, from the table of a diamond down to but not including the girdle. It refers to the portion of a brilliant-cut gemstone that is above the girdle.

Cubic crystal system—Also called the isometric crystal system. This is the system of crystals to which diamonds belong.

Diamond doublet—This is also known as an *assembled stone* and is basically junk. Often a doublet has a crown of diamond joined to a pavilion of some colorless stone. Sometimes a doublet consists of two pieces of diamond glued together.

Diamond lamp—Any lamp designed specifically for use when grading, or inside diamond display and sales cases, to show off the stones properly.

Diamond paper—A paper sheet folded in such a way that it will hold one or more diamonds without coming open. Often, information about the diamond or diamonds—such things as weight, prices, color, or clarity—are written on the front or a flap. The paper is usually durable. Often an inner liner of one or two sheets of thinner paper is used.

Diamond pipes—The core area where diamonds are found. From miles under the earth, where diamonds are created, a glob of diamond-carrying magma follows weaknesses in the crust of the earth until it gets near the surface. Pressure building from below forces the magma through the surface, creating a cone. Pipes are a diamond-bearing stream of rock, shaped somewhat like a carrot.

Diamond powder—An abrasive made of diamond dust. This material is sometimes referred to as diamond grit, and it consists of dust-like bits and the powder of diamonds. It is used for a variety of purposes. When affixed to the surface of some tools, it is used for machining, grinding, drilling, and so on. In the jewelry trade, it is used in faceting and polishing diamonds and is often used to fashion other hard gemstones.

Dispersion—The ability of transparent materials, including gems, to break white light into the spectral colors. The interval between the colors varies with the material, but dispersion is measured by the refractive indices of the rays of blue and red. Diamond's dispersion is .044. This is the highest dispersal reading of any colorless natural gem. Dispersion is one of the factors measured in determining whether a stone is actually a diamond. In the trade this quality is usually known as *fire*.

Dodecahedron—A rare but possible form of diamond crystals in the cubic crystal system. Technically speaking, stones of this configuration have a dozen rhomb-shaped faces. Each face intersects two of the crystal's axes and is parallel to the third.

Dop—A device used to hold a diamond (or any other gemstone) while it is being cut or polished. Dops are essentially handles that are attached to the stone to make it easier (or possible) to handle during the cutting, shaping, and polishing process.

Drawing color—The quality of a stone that gives it a visible body color due to the mechanics of light and reflection. The points on some cuts of stone are said to *draw color*, while the remainder of the stone may have no color visible to the naked eye. When more than one diamond is placed in a diamond paper and light passes through one stone into another, there is a tendency for color to be intensified. The selection of stones, seen under those light conditions, *draws color*.

Edge up—The position to hold a stone to best observe faint color tints. In this position the observer is looking at the diamond parallel to the plane of the stone's girdle.

Emerald cut—This is a *step cut* that enhances or brings out color in diamonds. It is characterized by rows, or *steps*, of long facets on the crown and pavilion, parallel to the girdle. There are usually steps on four sides of the stones, as well as at the corners where the sides join together. Usually, cutters place three steps on the crown and three on the pavilion, though the number may vary. Most cutters do not use an emerald or step cut for stones that have mid-range color since this type of cutting tends to bring out the traces of color. But the emerald cut is considered an excellent cutting style for fancy colored stones (which it will enhance the color of) or those in the colorless and near-colorless range (where it will have no effect). This cut dramatically reduces the fire or dispersion of a diamond. When cut in a square, it is known as a *square emerald cut*.

Enhanced diamond—A natural gem which has been altered in some way to improve its look. Color can be enhanced through heat, radiation, oils, and chemicals. This is often called a *treated stone.*

European cut—An older form of cutting that was never popularly adopted. It is based on mathematical formulae of light transmission and represents one of the first and more successful attempts to bring science into the cutting picture. But it is based on the light hitting the crown at a right angle, something that very seldom happens. For the curious, the table is 56 percent of the girdle diameter, the crown depth is 19 percent, and the pavilion depth is 40 percent. The pavilion facet angle relative to the girdle is 38° 40′; relative to the bezel angle it is 41° 6′.

Extra facets—Facets that are additional to those needed for the particular style of cut. These generally make the faceting asymmetrical, though the average nonprofessional would seldom notice. Extra facets are often added as a way of eliminating a minor blemish at or near the surface of a stone—such things as a nick or a *natural.*

Eye clean—A phrase that should make any buyer wary. A term used by many diamond dealers that is supposed to describe stock which a professional diamond grader, without using magnification, would find to be free of internal faults or flaws. *Eye perfect* is a variation of this term, meaning that the stone is free of both visible surface blemishes as well as internal flaws. In the real world, when someone uses these terms while trying to sell you a stone, it means that the stones have blemishes that are visible to a trained diamond grader but can be seen only with difficulty.

Facet—A polished surface, almost always on one of the many cleavage planes of a diamond.

Faceting—Placing facets on a diamond or other stone.

Face up—A position of the stone vis-à-vis the viewer in which the table is facing the viewer. This is the usual way in which mounted stones are seen. In diamonds the face-up position usually shows the least amount of color, and as a result when grading for color most diamond dealers use an edge-up or pavilion-up position.

Facing up well—A term that should serve as a warning whenever you're the purchaser. In the mid-range of color grades, a considerable number of diamonds that show signs of color in the edge-up position have no noticeable color when viewed face up. What usually happens is that the bright internal reflections of the light source mask the color tints.

False-colored diamond—A trade phrase used to describe diamonds that are slightly tinted with yellows but which fluoresce blue when viewed under natural light. A false-colored diamond looks better in natural light, where diamonds are usually graded, than they will when illuminated by incandescent light.

Fancy—A diamond with a body color tint that is so strong that it becomes an advantage rather than a liability. The most common fancy colors are yellow, green-yellow, brown, and black. Other colors are rarer but include orange, violet, green, blue, pink, and red.

Fancy cut, fancy shaped, moderne cut—Almost any cutting style other than the round brilliant or *single cut*. There are many different shapes. Become familiar with them as you learn: emerald cut, marquise cut, heart, pear, keystone, epaulet, half moon, triangle, etc.

Feather—A cleavage or fracture on a single plane within a stone. This type of flaw often has the appearance of a feather when it is viewed at a 90-degree angle to the cleavage plane.

File test—An old and discredited method of testing a stone to tell whether it is a diamond.

Finish—The quality of cutting, in addition to its proportions and the angles of the facets. Such things as the stone's polish, symmetry, smoothness of the girdle, size (or presence) of the culet, facet edge sharpness, and existence of extra facets are all items that are scrutinized when determining finish.

Fire—The word used widely in the diamond trade to describe the flashes of rainbow color that a diamond's facets give off, the result from dispersion. It is also referred to as *scintillation*. Fire can be seen when either the light source, the diamond, or the viewer moves.

Fisheye—A stone that is cut with a shallow pavilion. This alters the path of the light and the angles of reflection inside the diamond so significantly that the stone lacks brilliance and has a glassy look to it. This is the term given to the most glaring examples of what is also called a *shallow stone*.

Fissure—A long cavity in the surface of a diamond. This

cavity is often associated with a cleavage reaching the surface.

Flaw—An imperfection in a stone that lowers the value. Sometimes called a fault.

Flawless—A blemish-free diamond. Abbreviated to FL, the term means that no internal or external flaw can be seen by a trained and competent grader using a 10X loupe and correct lighting.

Fluorescence—The effect that physical properties of some stones have under certain wavelengths of light. The stone will cause some wavelengths that are visible and others that are invisible to the eye to change and be discernable in the visible range. Fluorescence can alter the color of a stone under certain conditions. For instance, an *overblue* exhibits a blue cast in the daylight but not under artificial light. A small but significant percentage of diamonds will fluoresce. Fluorescent diamonds should never be used as master stones for color grading.

Foil-backing—A method of simulating a diamond with faceted glass by using a thin sheet of metallic foil or reflective paint on the Pavilion of the stone. This increases the brilliancy of the piece to more closely resemble that of a diamond. Diamonds themselves are sometimes foil-backed, either to give a relatively clear stone a color or to improve the depth of color on a lightly tinted stone.

Four Cs—The diamond essentials: color, cut, clarity, and carat weight. This shorthand expression summarizes the major elements that go into valuation of a stone. For that reason, the Four Cs are critical for every diamond dealer to know and understand.

Fracture—A chip or break in a diamond in some direction other than a cleavage plane.

Girdle—The dividing line between the crown and pavilion of a diamond brilliant. This is the widest part of a stone in any direction and is what is grasped by the mounting or prongs. Well-cut Girdles have a waxy appearance. A bearded girdle is characteristic of a poorly cut stone and often consists of many small cracks at the outer edge of the diamond.

Girdle facets—Another name for break facets.

Girdle reflection—A visible warning of a badly cut diamond. In diamonds that have an extremely shallow pavilion, the girdle can be seen reflected in the table. Most buyers of quality stones see this as if it were a sign saying, "Don't bother with me."

Girdle thickness—The width of the girdle, measured perpendicular to the girdle's plane.

Goods—A common term among diamond professionals, with the possible exception of jewelers, for diamonds. Jewelers try to sell the mystique of diamonds to their purchasers. The others in the business know they are buying and selling a commodity, and the term is indicative of that.

Grain—The planes or directions in which it is easiest to cleave, saw, or polish a diamond. The most common usage of the term is for a diamond's cleavage direction.

Growth markings—These are markings characteristic of the diamond crystal's form. The vestiges of growth markings can sometimes be seen on a finished diamond's girdle; such markings are often used as one indication that the stone is, in fact, a diamond. Cubic diamonds show a square or rectangular marking. Triangular depressions are characteristic of octahedral diamond crystals. Finished stones made from dodecahedron-shaped crystals are grooved.

Halves—The usual term for a stone of about a half-carat—50 points, more or less.

Ideal cut—A diamond that has been cut in the brilliant fashion, with the size and shape of the facets designed to provide for a balance of maximum brilliance and dispersion. Also referred to as a *Tolkowsky cut* or *American cut*. This is the way a diamond is cut for the most beauty. However, many cutters, in order to increase carat weight and try to charge more for their finished stones, deviate from the ideal cut. Relatively few stones are actually cut to these standards.

Imperfect—Diamonds graded at the lower end of the gem scale. Imperfect as a rating refers to a diamond with a serious flaw that affects the durability of the stone or to a stone with flaws that are visible to the unaided eye when viewed face up.

Inclusion—Virtually any internal flaw except a fracture or cleavage, and some experts will include even these as inclusions. In its narrowest sense, it refers to any foreign object or visible crystal growth or graining inside a diamond.

Industrial diamonds—Diamonds that are not gem-quality stones, used for industrial purposes (e.g., in saws to cut stone and concrete) in bits for oil drilling, and in machine tools. Some better-grade industrials are cut and polished and sold as gem diamonds. Likewise, on occasion, a gem-quality stone may be used for specialized industrial purposes.

Internal strain—The strain and stress inside a diamond. These strains are often caused by an inclusion but can result from any number of distortions and irregularities of the structure. Internal strain can seriously affect the durability of a stone.

Jager—A top-quality diamond in one color classification system. The word is also used to describe a colorless stone that fluoresces blue (i.e., a stone that has a bluish cast in daylight but appears to be colorless under artificial light.)

Kimberlite—A type of peridotite that carries diamonds to the surface. This is often called blueground. Yellowground is blueground that has been badly weathered. In Australia a similar igneous type of rock is lamproite.

Kimberlite dike—A spike of plastic kimberlite that has been pushed up through the bedding planes of earlier rock and solidified. Diamonds are sometimes contained in such dikes.

Knife-edge girdle—The girdle of a stone that is excessively thin. Knife-edged girdles can be chipped easily.

Knot—A term applied to several different crystal conditions in a diamond. It generally indicates some type of included crystal in a stone, or a different orientation of the grain in one part of a diamond, that makes cutting and polishing difficult.

Limpid—An adjective describing a very transparent diamond that has no body color.

Loose goods—Diamonds that have been cut and polished but are not yet mounted in jewelry.

Lot—A term used a lot by diamond dealers. There are two similar but slightly different meanings. One is a group of rough stones offered to cutters by DeBeers at its diamond sights. The second use describes the arrangement of stones by color, cut, clarity, or some other attribute after they have been fashioned into gems.

Loupe—A small magnifying glass that will enlarge from 2X to 20X. The standard loupe used for grading diamonds is a 10X color-corrected loupe. Usually, loupes are designed to be worn in the eye or attached to glasses (eye loupe) or to be held in the hand (hand loupe). Both are used by professional jewelers, but most find that the eye loupe is preferable since it leaves both hands free to manipulate the diamond.

Louped—When the noun is turned into a verb it simply means that a stone has been examined under a loupe. This generally implies that it has been graded, but there are people who will suggest that when it is not true. The key here is to always find out what the speaker means.

Lumpy girdle—When a cutter produces a brilliant-cut diamond with an extremely thick girdle, the weight in points of a carat goes up. At the same time the quality goes down because the size of the girdle affects light reflections within the stone. This bit of tricksterism—designed to get someone to pay more because the stone weighs more—is related to a *thick stone.*

Luster—The stone's surface as it appears in reflected light. The quantity and quality of the light reflected from a well-cut diamond produce a readily identifiable luster.

Macle—This is a four-letter word in diamond cutting circles. It is a flattish, often triangular piece of diamond rough that for reasons relating to the way the crystal grew is difficult to fashion into a cut diamond. Most often, macles are used for fancy cuts since trying to get round brilliants out of them results in excessive wastage—when they can be properly cut at all. If you avoid doing business in diamond rough, you don't need to worry about this term, except insofar as someone will mention it in relationship to some fashioned stone. If you're buying rough, a macle should be purchased for considerably less than an equivalent-weight diamond that is not a macle.

Main facets—On a brilliant-cut stone these are virtually all the facets. This is a catch-all term for the crown and pavilion facets on a brilliant. On step-cut stones this term has a much narrower meaning; it refers to the center row facets on the pavilion.

Make—The finish and proportions, only, of a diamond. The positive comment is that the stone is "well made." Note that a stone of good make (i.e., well finished) could conceivably be riddled with included crystals and feathers, have poor color, etc. In other words, a seller can honestly say that a piece of junk he wants to sell you is well made just because the finish and proportions are nice.

Marquise—A fancy diamond shape that is close to the Brilliant in terms of the placement of facets. Often called *boat shaped*, it can best be thought of as a brilliant that has been stretched in one direction like a piece of silly putty.

Melange—One of the more important words in the diamond dealer's dictionary. Buyers of fashioned diamonds will generally be offered melange, a word that comes from the French and can be translated roughly as mixture. This is usually an assortment of stones, larger than .25 carat, in which the color, weight, or other factors are jumbled. Melange lots are not homogeneous, and they can be difficult to grade with any speed because there are few or no common characteristics of the stones.

Melee—These are small stones, up to about .25 carat in size. Single small stones are sometimes (incorrectly) referred to as melee when mounted as secondary stones to a main diamond. The diamond buyer will generally be dealing with melee in multiple-stone quantities.

Moe gauge—A device used to measure the width and depth of a brilliant-cut diamond, either mounted or unmounted. When used with a set of mathematical tables, it produces an approximation of the weight.

Mounted goods—Any diamonds that have been set in jewelry. This is particularly applied to, but not limited to, rings.

Mounting—A piece of metal or other material, often an amalgam of gold, silver, or platinum, designed to hold a diamond or other type of gem.

Natural—This is often the exception to the rule that an imperfection in a diamond lowers its value. A natural is a part of the diamond's original surface (and often triangular or square depressions within the natural are indicative that the stone is in fact a diamond). On some occasions, in order to get the most weight from rough, a jeweler will not polish the diamond's original surface off a fashioned stone. When the natural does not flatten the outline of the girdle, and when its lateral dimensions do not extend beyond the footprint for a medium-girdle, a natural is not regarded as a blemish. The existence of a natural on a girdle can be an important clue for the diamond trader in deciding whether a particular stone is a diamond.

Nick—Another name for a small-sized chip on a cut diamond. The most obvious place to look for nicks is along the girdle, although facet junctions and on a facet itself are other places where they are frequently found. Nicks can be caused by a slight blow to a diamond, from careless handling, and even from carrying several diamonds in a single diamond paper.

Off center—Both culets and tables, the smallest and the largest facets on a diamond, are sometimes off center. This is a sure indication of a badly cut diamond.

Off-center culets usually occur when a cutter attempts to fashion an odd-shaped piece of diamond rough and is unwilling to cut it to the right proportions and angles because of the extra weight he would have to lop off. When a culet is off center, the angles of opposing pavilion facets will be different, and incorrect, causing a loss of brilliance in the stone. Off-center tables are often the result of problems in cutting odd-shaped rough. To retain weight, some cutters will incline the table toward the girdle at some point, when it should be parallel at all points. Inevitably, crown facets on different sides of the stone will be cut at different angles, and the stone loses beauty.

Old European cut—A form of diamond cut no longer used and very seldom seen in most modern diamond transactions. It is the earliest type of full-cut, circular-girdled diamond brilliant. It is characterized by a high crown and small table. Many, many diamond professionals refer, mistakenly, to this cut as an *old mine cut*. The old mine cut has a squarish outline rather than a circular girdle.

Open culet—A culet that can be seen with the naked eye is flawed. If it can be seen without magnification it is too large for the purposes it is cut for—to protect the stone from damage at the bottom of the pavilion.

Out of round—A stone that is supposed to be a circular diamond brilliant but is not. An out-of-round stone is not a fancy shape; it is simply a stone that was supposed to be round but was cut lopsided.

Paperworn—When more than one diamond is carried in

a diamond paper the stones can rub or clink together. This sometimes causes scratches, or more often abraded facet edges, on the crown and pavilion.

Parcel—A group of diamonds offered for sale. It is used to mean any collection of diamonds, but in its most precise and accurate meaning it refers to diamonds that have been sorted and graded according to some common standard.

Paste—Any type of diamond imitation made out of glass.

Pavilion—That portion of the diamond below the girdle.

Pavilion main facets—The largest facets on the girdle, they run from the culet to the girdle on brilliant-cut stones. They are also called *bottom main* facets by some diamond dealers.

Pear cut—This is a 58-facet variation of the round brilliant. It qualifies as a fancy cut and is not an out-of-round diamond.

Perfect—A word usually overused in diamond dealings. Perfect stones are defined as having no imperfections or blemishes and no inferior cut or color that can be seen by a trained grader under a 10X loupe.

Pinks—One of the fancy-colored diamonds. In the trade, pink seems to refer to any stone with a hue that is red, purple, or violet.

Pique—A catch-all term that was supposed to mean diamonds with hard-to-see inclusions. It has been so misused over the years that many of the "grades" of pique actually are synonyms for poorer quality diamonds, those in the SI and I range. The term is often abbreviated in written documents to PK.

Point—One 100th of a carat.

Polish—The level to which the surface of the diamond is smoothed out in an effort to produce optical perfection. Under 10X magnification a quality polish should show no burn or wheel marks from the fashioning process. Any polish marks are usually grooves or scratches left on a facet.

Polished girdle—A diamond's girdle that has been faceted rather than smoothed. Sometimes called a faceted girdle.

Polishing—The process of turning diamond rough into a gem. Stages that are important for technical experts to know about include blocking and brillianteering.

Quarters—The usual term used by diamond dealers when referring to stones of about a quarter-carat, 25 points, more or less.

Red diamond—Diamonds with a color even approaching a ruby are virtually unheard of. When used by diamond merchants regarding a fancy-colored stone, *red diamond* generally refers to one that is rose colored or red-brown.

RI—The abbreviation of refractive index, the measure of how much light is bent when it enters or leaves a stone at an oblique angle. Generally, stones with high RIs are more brilliant.

Rough—Diamond crystals before they are cut, polished, and made into gemstones.

Rounding up—Part of the process of fashioning a rough stone into a gem; usually considered the part of the process by which the girdle outline is formed.

Rose cut—One of the oldest cuts of a diamond, it is still sometimes used on small diamonds. Beginning dealers always avoid this cut until they establish some definite need for it in their stocks. Probably first used by Indian cutters, the base is flat and unfaceted while the top is dome shaped and covered with a number of triangle-type facets.

Rough girdle—Much the same as a bearded girdle, although some diamond dealers use the term to describe a stone that does not have the hairline fractures at the girdle plane.

Scratches—One of the types of surface imperfections in a diamond. They are long, thin, and shallow (and usually rough edged).

Shallow stone—A diamond that has been cut in such a fashion that the pavilion-main facets are at an angle of less than 40 degrees to the plane of the girdle. A *fisheye* is the more extreme example of a shallow stone. Shallow stones generally have a glassy appearance.

Simulated diamonds—a type of manmade stone that is not a diamond or other gemstone at all. Although its color may be similar to that of a natural gem, it's very different physically and chemically.

Glass has been used in the past for diamonds, although today cubic zirconia is a well-known diamond simulation. These types of stones are often referred to as *simulants*.

Single cut—This form of cutting is often used with melee, or extremely small diamonds, where it would be difficult to cut and polish 52 facets. Sometimes erroneously referred to as a chip, the single cut is a circular-girdled stone that has a table, eight faces on the bezel, eight on the pavilion, and sometimes a culet.

Skin—The natural surface of an uncut diamond. When it is left unpolished on a stone's girdle, it is known as a natural.

Smalls—A term used by some diamond dealers to refer to stones of less than one carat but larger than melee.

Specific gravity—A figure that relates the weight and density of the diamond to that of water. It is usually abbreviated as SG. The SG of a diamond is 3.52.

Swindled stone—Cutting a wider than necessary table saves weight for the diamond cutter. Since it alters the angles of the stone's internal reflections, it cheats the customer of beauty. Actually, any deviation from the ideal of a 53-percent table will alter the reflection patterns, but diamond dealers seem unwilling to accept the ideal as a standard. They will maintain that a round brilliant diamond has not been swindled or spread until the table is equal to 60 to 65 percent (or sometimes more) of the girdle diameter. The felicitous-sounding phrase for an overly large table used among diamond professionals is *open table*. Some can even say "open table" in a way that makes a buyer think that is a positive attribute; it is not.

Star facets—On a brilliant-cut gem these are eight triangle-shaped facets along the edge of the table. They adjoin the main bezel facets.

Step cut—The other type of cutting besides the brilliant cut. In a step cut, all facets are in parallel rows above and below the girdle. All facets are quadrilaterals, and all except those that may be at corners are long. There are usually three rows of facets above the girdle and a similar number below the girdle on a step cut, although that is not a hard and fast rule.

Stone—A diamond or other gem. Diamond dealers usually refer to their goods as stones.

Symmetry—The care with which facets are placed opposite one another on a stone. In a symmetrical diamond, opposing facets are mirror images of one another.

Synthetic stones—Laboratory-grown stones that closely duplicate a natural gem's physical and chemical properties. These are the genuine item, though some diamond dealers don't like to admit that these are really diamonds. Synthetic industrial-grade diamonds were first synthesized in 1955; it wasn't until the 1980s that jewelry-grade diamonds were synthesized. These are not simulated diamonds or simulants. Synthetic diamonds are prized for their hardness, making them valuable for a variety of industrial uses, such as oil drilling.

Table—The large facet atop a faceted stone. On a brilliant-cut diamond, it has eight sides and is edged by the eight star facets.

Table down—The diamond as it appears when the Table is placed on a surface so that it can be viewed perpendicular to the pavilion facets. This is the most common position to use when grading for color. However, the edge-up position makes it easier to detect faint traces of color.

Table reflection—The size and shape of the table's reflection, when viewed on the pavilion facets through the top of the table, is a rough guide to whether the pavilion facets are cut at the proper angles.

Table size—Perhaps no single measurement can tell more about a stone than this one. The size is measured from one corner of the table to the opposing corner, not from edge to edge. It is expressed as a percentage in relationship to the girdle diameter. The best-proportioned stones have a table size of about 53 percent, but percentages much larger, sometimes 65 percent and more, are common. Although it is not always true, the fact that a stone has a table size near the ideal proportion often means that it has been cut with care by a professional who understands diamond proportions and respects them.

Thick crown—A characteristic that is seldom seen in modern cut stones is a stone with a thick crown—one that is deeper than 16.2 percent of the girdle diameter.

Thick stone—When a fashioned stone is cut deep, rather

than to correct proportions, the angles of the various facets are changed, the path of the reflections within the gem are changed, and the stone loses brilliance. Some unscrupulous diamond cutters will intentionally produce this type of stone. These people effectively are trying to get more from the rough than is legitimately there. Also sometimes called a *lumpy stone*.

Thirds—Stones of approximately one-third carat. For some reason, diamond dealers will use the term most often when they are on the lower side of .33 carats.

Tolkowsky cut—The scientifically based cut of a round brilliant-cut diamond using the laws of physics that produce maximum brilliancy of a stone consistent with high degrees of fire. Using the average size of the girdle as 1, a stone cut to Tolkowsky specifications has.

- total depth 59.3 percent,
- crown depth 16.2 percent,
- pavilion depth 43.1 percent,
- girdle depth 1 (larger stones) to 3 percent,
- table size 53 percent,
- bezel angle 34° 30', and
- pavilion angle 40° 45'.

Treated diamond—A stone that has been treated, often with heat or a coating, to improve the appearance or color.

MEASURING FOR WEIGHT

Weight is one of the most important factors affecting a diamond's value. Measurements of a diamond's size, taken with a screw micrometer, can be converted into fairly accurate estimations of its weight.

Estimating weights is a dangerous thing to do—but sometimes you may have no other alternative. For that reason I'll include a couple of formulae that may be useful. But keep in mind that these figures are approximations and will not yield the exact weight.

Some of the more widely accepted formulae for estimating weight from physical measures are listed below. The key measurements when measuring a diamond are the depth and the diameter. When you're dealing with unmounted stones, it's fairly easy to get those figures and plug them into a formula. When dealers are handling mounted stones, there's a lot of guesstimating that goes on in the diamond trade, but in the smuggling business, *no one ever* deals with mounted goods. They know that's among the fastest ways to get ripped off.

Despite the fact that relying on the estimated weight of stones is not a good idea, particularly if you have a scale available, it is worthwhile to make estimates in all cases. The estimates may be usable later. And estimating the weight of the stone from the measurements is sometimes useful. A correctly estimated weight that appears to be out of line with the actual weight, as determined from a diamond balance, is a pretty good indicator that the whole transaction should be reviewed carefully to see if some sort of diamond substitute is being palmed off as the genuine article.

When measuring the diameter of brilliants (round stones), keep in mind that few diamonds are perfectly circular. For that reason, look carefully at the stone to see where the maximum and minimum girdle diameters are, measure each, and average the two.

In fancy cuts the term diameter is a little trickier. The general rule here is that diameter means length—the stone's longest dimension—and width—generally the longest dimension at right angles to the length.

There are some exceptions to these rules, however, and they're worth knowing about, though you'll seldom need them. The length of heart-shaped diamonds is the distance between an imaginary line drawn across the tops of the lobes to the tip of the point. Call the width the widest part of the lobes. When measuring a triangle cut (another one that's wise to stay away from when purchasing), measure the width first. If all sides of the triangle are equal, any side can be measured at the width. If the sides are not equal, call the width the distance along either the shortest or longest side, from corner to corner. The length of the triangle cut is then measured along a line that is perpendicular to the side you chose as the width, from that side to the point opposite it.

When using a screw micrometer, use one that measures in millimeters; if you use one that measures in the English system, the following formulae are wrong, wrong, WRONG.

Most important, remember that any time you are using a micrometer to determine dimensions, avoid tightening the screw once the stone is resting between the jaws. Diamonds can be damaged easily, and clamping down hard is an excellent way to hurt a stone.

WEIGHT ESTIMATION FORMULAE

Round brilliant:
Estimated weight = Average diameter squared x depth x .0061

Oval brilliant:
Estimated weight = Average diameter squared x depth x .0062

Heart-shaped brilliant:
Estimated weight = Length x width x depth x .0059

Triangular brilliant:
Estimated weight = Length x width x depth x .0057

B

CONCEALMENT

THERE ARE INNUMERABLE PLACES TO CONCEAL DIA-MONDS, GEMS, AND OTHER CONTRABAND IN BUILDINGS, VEHI-CLES, OR ON YOURSELF. The possible places are limited only by imagination. However, government agents are taught a list of the "most likely" locations where contra-band will be concealed, and that list serves as a floor for searches of homes, cars, and people. More inventive agents consider the list a floor and try to imagine other locations where items can be stashed. Some agents con-sider the list a ceiling and don't search beyond it—if they even search all these places.

Take this list—distributed by a U.S. government agency to its operatives—for what it is. Be aware that customs and other agents the world over probably have similar lists, ones that may be either a "floor" or a "ceil-ing" during searches. The listing is as distributed by fed-eral agents.

HOMES, BUILDINGS, AND LUGGAGE ITEMS

Telephone base and handle
Sealed cigarette package
Inside and under wigs
Under washbowl, sink, or tub
Base of lamp
Closet clothing—waistbands, pens in pockets, sleeves, hatbands, shoes, gloves
Flower pots and window boxes
Wall and ceiling light fixtures
Prescription bottles
Mattresses
Behind picture frames, posters, or mirrors
Flashlights
Removable air conditioning registers
Pet box
Light switches
Behind baseboards
Inside hollow doors (removable top)
Under carpets
Inside hollow curtain rods and closet rods, shower curtain rods
Inside stairway posts
Inside door chimes and doorbell
Inside deep-well fryers
Range hoods and filters
Rolled-up window shades
Mailbox
Inside knife handles
Behind wall phones
Inside transistor radio
Hanging out window
Sink traps

Dog collars
Refrigerator: underneath fruits, vegetables, meat; taped
  under door, motor compartment.
Furniture upholstery
Inside toilet tanks
Magazines and books
Bedposts
Musical instruments and cases
False bottom on radiator covers
All kitchen canisters and containers
Doorknobs
Behind walls
Hung behind curtains
Inside TV and radio sets
Inside false ceilings and chimneys
Plumbing inspection doors
Inside crucifix
Golf bags
Test tubes
Inside cameras
Taped to top of toilet bowl
Window ledge next door
In floor drain
False aerosol cans
Fluorescent light tubes
Toys and stuffed animals and games
In Band-aids and Band-aid boxes
Top of window, door sills, moldings
Fire and water hoses
Cellar beams
Venetian blinds—top and bottom
Inside clocks
Child's bank
Agitator of washer

Chandelier
Inside trophies
Inside rolled-up newspaper
Electrical socket
Stick deodorant containers
Cold cream and petroleum jelly jars
Taped in dressers and behind drawers
Inside ceramic and clay figurines
Inside candlestick holders
Inside handle of carpenter's toolbox
Taped to movable clotheslines
Inside pipe rack stand
Behind exterior brick near window
Rifle barrel buttplate
Inside rifle cartridge and shotgun shell
Inside tinfoil tubing roll
Zippered cushions and pillows
Under panel of parquet floor
Inside toilet bowl float
Fuse box
Fish tanks and bowls
Hollow soap cakes
Top edge of doors
Hollowed-out furniture legs
Salt and pepper shakers
Hollowed fruits and vegetables
Record albums
Spice jars
Wax paper dispensers
Magnet boxes
Fire alarm bell
False-bottom baby carriage and cribs
Douche bags
Doghouses

Footlockers
35mm film cans
Within sanitary napkins and in box
Rain gutters and drain spouts
Hot-air ducts
Hem of drapes and curtains
Hidden in box of mattress frame
Hollowed-out tree
Shoe polish container and equipment
Razor blade dispenser
Stovepipes
Garbage bags
Pillowcases
Furnace
Seams of field cots and hollow cap of cot legs
Attic insulation
Inside hassock
Hidden drawers in tables
Inside TV tube
Inside color TV antenna
Inside abandoned plumbing
In tool box
Inside letters
Inside and behind vacuum cleaner bags
Inside handle of vacuum cleaners
Inside room dividers
Inside patch-trap of antique rifle
Inside Christmas tree decorations
Behind kick plates of sink cabinets
Conduit from fuse box
Jewelry box
Clothes hamper
In stove insulations and stove exhausts and drip pans
Under lip ring of plastic trash cans

In toothpaste tubes
In surfboards
In electric toothbrush holders
Talcum and cold cream containers
Tea bags
Acoustical tile ceiling
Holy Bible (hollow cover)
Baked bread, cookies, and brownies
Cookies and candy bars
Art kits
Dolls
Fuel-oil heaters
Psychedelic light housing
Hollowed-out flashlight batteries
Hollowed-out pad of paper
Seltzer antacid
Base of rabbit ears antenna
In eggs
Mixed with tobacco
Taped to hatboxes
Leg of bathtub
Toaster tray
Plastic rolling pin
Razor blade disposal slot
Shower head nozzle
Chimney clean out
Hair dryer
Clock
Hollow cane
Pay telephone coin return
Under corner of mailbox
Shaving brush handle
Miniature chessboards
Behind and inside medicine cabinets

In clothesline pipe
Ironing board legs
Bottom half of double boiler
Typewriters, computers, and covers

AUTOMOBILE

Dome, headlights, and taillights
Hubcaps
Inside horn
Air filter
Oil filter
Spare tire—treads and well
Windshield washer fluid container
Shift knobs
Instrument panel and ornamental objects on dashboard
Cars with double sunroofs
Ashtrays, in and under
Picnic jug in trunk
False battery
Under brake and gas pedals
Frame
License plate
False heater hoses; heater
Sun visors
Under rugs
Upholstery
Behind bumpers
False dual muffler
Hollow voltage regulator
Heater
Vents (air and heater)
Radio speaker grill
On top of gas tank (suspended or concealed in compartment)

Glove compartments—top of compartment or trap
Convertible tops
False bottom of trunk beds
Fuse box
Backseat
Floorboard
Trunk
Inside oil cap
Hide-a-Key
Under seats
Cigarette lighter
Carburetor
Pill vials
Under tire air-valve caps
Inside motorcycle handlebar tubing
Compartment under floor of older Volkswagen cars
Inside tubing on roof rack
Inside auto surfboard racks
Motorcycle taillights
Rocker panels
Tailpipe
Insulation under hood
Taxicab roof light
Under chrome
Key case
Taped to window
Service station travel kits
False radios, stereos, CD players
Under side of fender
Armrest
Inside flashlight
Tied to axle

CONCEALMENT

ON PERSON

Lipstick tube
Cigarette lighter and packs
Taped under breast or brassieres
Processed hair, hair buns, and wigs
Rectum
Vagina
Nose
Ears
Mouth
Cheeks of buttocks
Lapel of jackets and coats
Inside and back of watch and other jewelry
Taped behind ears
Cuffs and waistbands
Pockets
Shoes and socks
Pill vials
Inside sanitary napkins or tampons
Hat band
35mm film cans
Baby's diapers
Corsets
Under false teeth
Slit belts or zippered belts
Belt buckles
Behind collars and collar stays
Foreskin of penis
Under bandages
False limbs
Glass eyes
Hearing aid Glasses
Jock straps

Swallowed, with string to teeth
Between toes and taped to feet
Tie knot of necktie, handkerchiefs
Wallet
Eyeglass case
Contact lens case
Inside pens and pencils
Tobacco tins or pouches
Money belts
Lining of clothing
Hollow end of cane or umbrella handle
In gum sticks
Cigarette filters
Compact
Casts
In addressed envelopes
False buttons
In male girdle
In swim trunks
In stem of pipe
In gum stuck behind ear
Pinned to shorts
Inside identification bracelets
Inside feces bag
Inside hollowed-out crutches
Inside neck and wrist lockets, bracelets, and charms
Rings
Earrings
Tie pins, clasps, and cuff links
Fountain pens
Inside fly flap of trousers
Battery box of hearing aid
Thermos jug
Liners of luggage

Canteens
Inhalers
Lining of change purse
Under insulation in motorcycle helmet
Military cap insignia, lapel, and shoulder patches

DEALING WITH DIAMOND PAPERS

THERE IS LITTLE THAT WILL GIVE YOU AWAY AS A NEO-PHYTE FASTER THAN MISHANDLING PACKETS OF DIAMONDS. Folding a diamond packet is an art akin to closing up a road map. And opening one is an art form in its own way.

It's such a small thing, but the way that you handle a diamond packet—the way you open it and close it—will tell the person you're with that you're a pro or will warn him that you don't have a clue.

You'll want to buy diamond papers and inner liners from a jewelry supply store, but for a first effort you can use a piece of typing paper. The procedure is as follows:

1. Cut it into a piece about 7.25 inches long by 5.5 inches wide. This approximates one of the common sizes of paper.

2. Lay it on the table, with the longer dimension parallel to you. The first time you do this, mark an X on the paper, about .25 inch from the top of the paper and

halfway across the width. That will help orient you in the rest of the folding process, but it is not normally part of folding a diamond paper.

3. Measuring from the top of the paper, crease the paper 4.50 inches down the "page." Fold the bottom flap up so that what was previously the bottom edge is parallel to the top edge. The X should still be visible above the folded-up edge.

4. Fold the right side of the paper toward the left, creasing it when it extends about 1.25 inches over central portion. The X should still be visible.

5. Fold the left side of the paper toward the right, creasing it when it extends about 1.25 inches over the central portion. You have formed a pocket with the paper. The X should still be visible.

6. Fold the top of the pocket downward. Crease the paper about 1.50 inches from the bottom. The X will no longer be visible. You will now see a square of paper, but the flaps and the pocket you formed previously will not be visible.

7. Turn the piece of paper over so that the side flaps and pocket are visible. The X will be visible again.

8. Fold the top edge down so that it overlaps the bottom. This will be the top flap. The X will no longer be visible. You now have a properly-folded diamond packet that is approximately 3 by 1.5 inches.

To open up the folded packet, do the following:

1. Hold the paper with both hands. The front, or top, of the folded diamond paper should be facing you, with the only uncreased or open edge of the packet closest to your body.

2. Lift the top flap up with a thumb.

3. Fold the bottom flap downward.

4. Determine where the stone is located in the packet by feeling the paper and finding the lump.

5. Open one of the side flaps.

6. Tilt the paper in such a way as to get the diamond inside to move toward a bottom corner or crease. You may want to tap the edge of the paper lightly to help move the stone.

7. Carefully open the other side flap.

8. Put your finger inside one of the open flap side and carefully fold down the bottom flap. *Carefully.* At this point there is nothing to hold the stone inside the paper and it could easily pop out onto the floor or table or into a fold in your clothes.

9. When you are finished examining the stone, but it back in the middle section of the paper and fold as before, bringing up the bottom edge so that it is parallel to the top edge, etc.

ABOUT THE AUTHOR

Maximillian S. Callahan is a professional who declines to state his business or background or have a picture of himself published. You will understand why once you read this book.